Women and the Liberator

BY William P. Barker

    Twelve Who Were Chosen
    They Stood Boldly
    Everyone in the Bible
    Who's Who in Church History
    Saints and Swingers
    Women and the Liberator

WILLIAM P. BARKER

Women and the Liberator

MONROEVILLE UNITED METHODIST
CHURCH LIBRARY

Fleming H. Revell Company
Old Tappan, New Jersey

Unless otherwise identified, Scripture quotations in this volume are from the *Revised Standard Version of the Bible*, copyrighted 1946 and 1952.

Scripture references identified NEB are from *The New English Bible*. © The Delegates of the Oxford University Press and the Syndics of the Cambridge University Press 1961 and 1970. Reprinted by permission.

Scripture references identified TEV are from the Today's English Version of the New Testament. Copyright © American Bible Society 1966.

Acknowledgments

A special appreciation must be expressed to several persons who consciously or unconsciously collaborated on this book. I am grateful to the women in my own life: Jean, my wife; Ellen, my daughter; Mrs. John B. Barker and Mrs. Jarvis M. Cotton, mother and mother-in-law respectively—all of whom shared valuable insights. Also to Jock, my son; to Fred M. Rogers and the Luxor Ministerial Association; to Mrs. D. Wayne Fraker, who typed the manuscript; and to colleagues in the Pittsburgh Theological Seminary community go my sincere thanks.

ISBN 0-8007-0518-1 cloth

ISBN 0-8007-0530-0 paper

Copyright © 1972 by Fleming H. Revell Company
All Rights Reserved
Library of Congress Catalog Card Number: 73-186532
Printed in the United States of America

TO
Maisie and Douglas McKenzie

Contents

Introduction		9
THE JEWISH MOTHER	(Mary, Mother of Jesus)	15
THE WIDOW	(Anna)	28
THE SUPERMOM	(Salome)	33
THE CALL GIRL	(Woman Who Was a Sinner)	41
THE TEEN-AGER	(Jairus's Daughter)	48
THE UNWANTED	(Woman With a Hemorrhage)	55
THE WEEPER	(Widow of Nain)	62
THE TIRED HOUSEWIFE	(Woman Unable to Stand Straight)	70
THE SEXUAL OBJECT	(Woman of Samaria)	76
THE FUSSER	(Martha)	83
THE UNAPPRECIATED	(Mary of Bethany)	91
THE EXECUTIVE'S WIFE	(Joanna)	100
THE SOCIALITE	(Pilate's Wife)	109
THE NEUROTIC	(Mary Magdalene)	123

Introduction

Jesus is the Emancipator. There had never been anyone who appreciated the personhood of women as he did. There has never been anyone like him since.

Primitive societies subjected women to a position verging on slavery. The women bore the children abundantly, reared them, kept the hut in repair, gathered the food in woods and streams and fields, cooked, cleaned, made all the clothing, carried the goods if the tribe moved. When the natives of the Lower Murray first saw pack oxen of the earliest settlers, they thought these were the wives of the whites. "Women," intoned a chief of the Chippewas, "are created for work. One of them can draw or carry as much as two men. They are also able to pitch our tents, make our clothes, mend them, and keep us warm at night.... We absolutely cannot get along without them on a journey. They do everything and cost only a little; for since they must be forever cooking, they can be satisfied in lean times by licking their fingers."

Women were bought in marriage exactly as animals or slaves. They were bequested as property when their husbands died. In certain cultures (New Guinea, India, Fiji, the New Hebrides, the Solomon Islands) widows were strangled and buried, or forced to commit suicide in order to attend their man in the next life. Men were nearly always permitted to have sexual license, while women were expected to practice complete fidelity. The double standard was commonplace.

Even in more developed civilizations, women were relegated to an inferior place. Periclean Greece, for all of its culture, granted little dignity to married women. Socrates invited Aspasia, a professional courtesan, to discuss how she might ply her trade with a maximum profit.

Earlier, the great Homer, looking up from his wine bowl, advised "No trust is to be placed in women." Aristotle, revealing his own inner lack of security, wrote, "Women may be said to be inferior to man." In Rome about 215 B.C., the illustrious Cato the Censor, betrayed his male chauvinism, remarking, "Suffer women to arrive at an equality with you and they will from that moment become your superiors."

Babylon, cradle of so much enlightenment in law, medicine, astronomy and physics, also degraded women. The Babylonians' penal code, a model of jurisprudence in so many ways, decreed that if a man repudiated his wife, he must pay her one-half mina and be free. "If a woman repudiates her husband," the code also provided, "she shall be drowned in the river."

Buddha, who deserted his wife and was always uncomfortable in the presence of women, hesitated long before finally admitting them into the Buddhist order. His favorite disciple once asked him. "How are we to conduct ourselves, Lord, with regards to womenkind?"

"As not seeing them, Ananda," Buddha replied.

Islam permits plural marriage with up to four wives, and Mohammed himself had almost three times that number. Many Moslems interpret the Koran, Surah IX, verse 28 to permit temporary alliances for men away from home on business, or at war. The marriage bond with any wife may be dissolved at will by the husband, according to Islam. The reason why the initiative lies with the man in Koranic law was summed up by the president of the Moslem board of elders in Jerusalem: "Since the man is sounder in judgment and more capable of self-control and the one to pay the alimony, Islam has given him the right to dissolve the marriage . . . the woman is liable to abuse such a right since she is temperamentally and emotionally unstable."

The Code of Manu, the Brahman Law in India advised sternly, "The source of dishonor is woman, the source of strife is woman, the source of earthly existence is woman; therefore, avoid woman." Among the Chinese, perhaps the most civilized people of the time, custom backed by law reduced women to a humiliating position. A woman who disobeyed her husband was believed to become a jackal in her next incarnation. If too many daughters were born and times were hard, the infant girls might be abandoned in the fields to die of exposure or be eaten by prowling animals. Women lived in separate quarters, never mingling with the men. The poet Fu Hsuan sang,

> How sad is it to be a woman!
> Nothing on earth is held so cheap.

Hebrew woman, although not reduced to the level of man's beast of burden or plaything, nevertheless was relegated to second-class citizenship. In the great temple in Jerusalem, women could not pass beyond the Court of the Woman. The more sacred inner precincts were for males only. Summing up woman's place, the Sayings of the Jewish Fathers states, "Her work is to send her children to be taught in the synagogue, to attend to domestic concerns, to leave her husband free to study in the schools, to keep house for him until he returns."

The church has never caught up with Jesus. In spite of the auspicious start where its corporate life reflected the truth that ". . . there is neither male nor female; for you are all one in Christ Jesus" (Galatians 3:28), by the third century, A. D., the church fell into its own kind of double standard. St. Anthony, retiring to the desert, introduced a rigorous asceticism with antifeminist overtones. In reading the accounts of poor Anthony's temptations, one need not be a Freudian to detect his covert sexual fantasies. The writings of other Christian hermits and monastics reveal a blushingly blatant preoccupation with women as sexual objects. In effect, they syllogistically thought, sin is rooted in desire; the cause of all sexual desire is women; therefore, the devout man must remove himself from all contact with the noxious source of evil. This streak of antifeminism has stained all subsequent theology, and the church never has quite rinsed it out.

Even the Reformers carried over into their writings the then-prevalent condescending attitude toward women. Martin Luther warned his followers, "What defects women have, we must check them in private, gently by work of mouth, for woman is a frail vessel."

John Calvin, before his marriage, writing to a friend stipulated the qualities he admired in a wife, "The only comeliness that attracts me is this: that she be modest, complaisant, unostentatious, thrifty, patient, and likely to be careful of my health." Sometime later, after his wife's death, he wrote another friend admitting his grief and eulogizing his wife as one from whom he "never experienced the slightest hindrance."

Stormy Scotsman John Knox, criticizing the rule of Mary Tudor in 1558, wrote a tract with the resounding title, "First Blast of the Trumpet Against the Monstrous Regiment of Women." In it he denounced attempts to promote any woman ("weak, frail, impatient, feeble, and foolish creatures") to any position of authority as the "subversion of good order, of all equity and justice," as well as contrary to God and repugnant to nature!

In Colonial New England, saturated with Free Church Puritanism, it was customary for the church bell to toll six times when a woman died. A man was worth nine. Samuel Johnson, the embodiment of eighteenth century Protestant enlightenment, was once asked his opinion of giving women a more prominent voice in the church. "Sir," the great man huffed, "a woman preaching is like a dog's walking on his hind legs. It is not done well, but you are surprised to find it done at all."

Among many in the church today, this is still the prevailing attitude. Witness the fact the ordination is still withheld from women in many branches in the church.

Dorothy Sayers, writer of detective stories and theological essays once astutely observed, "Perhaps it is no wonder that the women were first at the Cradle and the last at the Cross. They had never known a man like this man—there has never been such another."

In this age of hot and cold running Lib movements, we need to behold The Liberator. What better way than through the eyes of the women who were given freedom by him? The accounts which follow are an attempt to look at Jesus through the eyes of the liberated women around him.

WILLIAM P. BARKER

Women and the Liberator

THE JEWISH MOTHER
(Mary, Mother of Jesus)

Blessed art Thou, O Lord our God, King of the Universe, Who has not made me a woman (Mishnah, Peah, Chapter I).

Mary had heard her father, a devout Jew, pray this ancient prayer each morning for as long as she could remember. She had quickly learned that every Jewish male intoned these words each day after waking, thanking God that he had been born a man.

When Mary went to the synagogue, she and her mother sat in the tiny balcony, screened off by latticework and located to one side from the main room where the men gathered. The girl quickly sensed her place. In God's scheme, she surmised, women were born an inferior species.

The village boys attended the synagogue classes to study *Torah*. Mary, who had a deep reverence for Yahweh and the story of His dealings with Israel, sometimes envied them for their opportunity to learn to read and discuss that story. However, she obediently followed her mother's instructions, learning the hundreds of domestic skills which every Galilean housewife had to know.

When a girl was one day past her twelfth birthday, she was legally a woman. She was also eligible as a bride. In fact, if she was not betrothed within a reasonable time, she grew apprehensive. She knew that an unmarried girl soon acquired a stigma.

Painfully shy and profoundly religious, Mary kept her apprehensions to herself. She brightened, however, when a village craftsman-carpenter named Joseph indicated that he would like to initiate the steps leading to marrying her. Joseph, Mary knew, carried the reputation of being a man of immense integrity. Furthermore, Mary had heard that Joseph conscientiously practiced his faith.

In spite of her feelings of inadequacy, Mary began to live in that lavender mixture of fantasy and reality in which every bride exists before the wedding. The last thing the young woman expected was the announcement from a messenger from God.

". . . You will conceive in your womb and bear a son, and you shall call his name Jesus. He will be great, and will be called the Son of the Most High; and the Lord God will give to him the throne of his father David, and he will reign over the house of Jacob for ever; and of his kingdom there will be no end" (Luke 1:31–33).

Not knowing whether to cry or cheer, Mary accepted the responsibility. "I am the Lord's servant," (Luke 1:38 TEV), she sighed, saying that she understood that she was the "handmaid" or female slave for God. Carrying a baby out of wedlock, especially in a prudish place like her home village, Mary knew, meant being ostracized by the other women. Worse, Mary feared that Joseph would break off the plans for marriage. Mary wondered why the Lord laid such impossible burdens on her. Conscious that she would always be God's slave, Mary resolved that she would try to obey.

Mary lived with bewilderment and anxiety most of her life. Years later, she remembered the perplexity of her pregnancy and the remarkable understanding Joseph showed. She recalled the tiring journey to Bethlehem in her ninth month, her fright when labor pains began, her uneasiness when Joseph helped her into the tiny cave where the animals were sheltered. Mary thought of the miracle and mystery of birth, and how close God had seemed at the time her baby was born. Later she longed to describe to Joseph her sense of God's presence when she was delivering. She felt, however, that she never could adequately express her feelings, and she noticed that Joseph always looked as if he could not quite grasp what she was talking about.

Mary locked up other womanly secrets in her mind's memory chest. She recalled the strange visit of the group of eastern sages and their expensive gifts for Jesus. With a recollection of the horror, she also remembered the night when Joseph wakened her, urgently whispering that they would have to flee at once because Herod, the crazy ogre ruling the area, had heard rumors about her "kingly" son's birth and intended to slay all baby boys in the vicinity. Mary had wept for the other mothers near Bethlehem who had not been able to grab their babies and rush across the border to safety. It seemed to Mary that God had somehow intended her baby to carry out the plans which the Messenger had announced ten or eleven months earlier. Life, Mary thought, was bewildering. Nonetheless, she felt grateful.

When Herod died and it was safe to return home, Mary and Joseph stopped at Jerusalem to express their thanks at the temple. Normally, forty-one days after the first baby was born, parents tried to visit the Jerusalem temple to offer up a gift, symbolizing the purification of the mother and the presentation of the firstborn to the Lord. It was customary to sacrifice a lamb at the temple. For the very poor, a pigeon had to suffice. Joseph and Mary revealed their poverty by buying a pigeon. In spite of their meager purse, however, they determined to show their gratitude to God for the gift of their baby, Jesus.

Poverty and piety seemed to be the chief characteristics of their home in Nazareth, but Mary never complained. Her days were filled with the never ending round of wifely chores—cooking, washing, sweeping, baking, fetching water, grinding grain for flour, shopping, tending children. She patiently bore a typically large Palestinian family—four other boys besides Jesus and at least two girls.

Nazareth, a six-hour donkey ride from Haifa on the Mediterranean on one side and the same distance from Tiberius on Galilee on the other side, was a typical peasant village, and Mary was a typical Jewish peasant mother. Devout but poor, she was unable to afford anything but porous pottery and could never buy a set of separate utensils for the correct "clean" ritualistic food preparation. Mary knew that to be poor was to be labeled a "sinner," in the eyes of the self-righteous purists. Nevertheless, she taught each baby, beginning with Jesus, the "Now I Lay Me Down To Sleep" for Jewish children, the haunting words of Psalm 31:5 which begins with, "Into thy hands I commit my spirit." Faithfully, each Sabbath, Mary carried and led her brood to the women's section of the Nazareth synagogue. Sometimes nursing the youngest and occasionally reproving her other youngsters for squirming, she set them an example, listening to the thirty-five to forty verses of the Law read in Hebrew and translated immediately into Aramaic.

Mary sometimes felt perplexed by her eldest, Jesus. She noted how independent and self-reliant he seemed to be. When she mentioned her apprehensions to her husband, Joseph dismissed them with a smile, pointing out that their son was growing up.

Mary's face shone with pride when Jesus at twelve became a *bar mitzvah*, taking on the obligations of a son of the Law. That year, she and Joseph had decided to take Jesus to Jerusalem for Passover. Mary relived the last journey south when she had been carrying her unborn child, and pondered how quickly the years had sped. At the same time, she found herself caught up in the bustle and excitement of joining a group of pilgrims to the Holy City. When the group reached Jerusalem, Mary proudly watched her husband and son go together to the temple. Jesus, she noted, seemed so adult.

The time came to return to Nazareth, and Mary, the smaller children and the other women and their offspring started out early in the day. Inasmuch as the women and children traveled more slowly and required more frequent rest stops, the men and the older boys usually lingered in the city until later in the day, then caught up with the womenfolk in time for the evening meal. Mary, therefore, did not worry when she did not notice Jesus in her group. She assumed that he would come along later with Joseph.

Joseph, on the other hand, did not find Jesus with the men when he departed, and took it for granted the young Jesus had decided to accompany the women earlier in the day. When Joseph joined Mary late in the day and did not find Jesus, he was as agitated as Mary. He tried to allay her fears and assured her that he and she would return immediately at daybreak to Jerusalem.

When they finally found their twelve-year-old boy in the temple precincts listening to a dialogue between some of the learned elders, Mary and Joseph felt a sense of relief. At the same time, they were irked. Mary fussed at Jesus for causing them such anxiety. "Son," she scolded, "why did you do this to us? Your father and I have been terribly worried trying to find you" (Luke 2:48 TEV).

When she heard his reply that they should have known that he had to be in his Father's house, Mary was so startled that she found herself speechless. What did Jesus mean? she wondered. These words from the lips of her own boy had overtones of some special relationship to God. Then she remembered the words of the announcement by the angel. Why couldn't her son be like other twelve-year-olds and think about games and chums? Mary fretted.

During the next years, Mary often worried about her firstborn. She couldn't understand why he liked to go on long walks into the hills by himself, why he seemed to be given to deep periods of silence.

At the same time, Mary felt grateful that Jesus worked diligently with Joseph whenever Joseph worked. When Joseph's death left her widowed and desolate, Mary appreciated her son's understanding and comfort. She noticed, too, that Jesus quietly stepped into Joseph's role of family provider. With a feeling of relief, she sensed that her strange oldest son would look after her and the younger children.

Mary's perplexity about Jesus returned, however, when her other sons grew large enough to help as breadwinners. She observed how Jesus seemed restless. She said nothing when he announced one evening that he planned to leave in the morning to go down to the Jordan for several days. Mary knew without asking that he intended to hear his cousin, John the Baptizer. Although she did not mind Jesus listening to John the Baptizer, Mary had heard rumors that John the Baptizer was under surveillance. Mary did not want her son getting into any scrapes. Galilee, Mary knew, seethed with political plots. Roman garrisons kept a wary watch everywhere. Mary could never forget the ghastly sight of helpless Galilean boys crucified along the roadside by the Romans for complicity in some anti-Roman movement. Protective mother that she was, Mary determined that her son not be victimized by the Roman overlords.

Mary's apprehensions grew after Jesus returned from John the Baptizer's camp meeting. She noticed that her son had a sense of purpose about him. She also observed that he began to preach. His preaching, she quickly caught, was not the bland platitudes of a timid young rabbi, but a ringing demand for repentance, because of the coming of God's Kingdom, a new age. She remembered that years earlier, before his birth, the heavenly announcer had told her that her son would be a great ruler with a unique mission. She had never been able to sort out the meanings of words in that message.

Mary could not understand her son's talk about "the Kingdom" or the new age. Once at the neighboring village of Cana, she thought she caught a glimpse of what he meant when he presented a sign or object lesson during a wedding feast.

Mary was the caterer, in charge of the serving. To Mary's dismay, the refreshments gave out. Unexpected numbers of guests—including Jesus and his coterie of friends—had shown up. For Mary it was a crisis. Not to have a sufficient supply of beverage on hand was an unforgivable, unforgettable breach of hospitality. The bride and groom, Mary knew, would never be able to live down the humiliation.

Flustered and upset, Mary rushed toward Jesus. It was an emergency, she signalled. She pleaded with him to do something, immediately, to help everybody out of the awkward situation. Although Mary had confidence that her son could handle the situation, she fussily tried to manage him.

In spite of Mary's too-eager prompting, Jesus patiently put his mother at ease. He then instructed some of the other helpers to fill the six big stone jars usually used for the ceremonial cleanings with water. Later, he ordered some of the contents of the first jar to be taken to the master of ceremonies.

The guest serving as the master of ceremonies, unaware of the crisis in the kitchen, had been busy making toasts, keeping the party lively and helping everyone feel welcome. He and the others had already imbibed enough to begin to relax and have a good time. The master of ceremonies, not knowing of Jesus' intervention, took a sip of the new supply and announced that it was tastier than anything served up until then. Laughingly, he pointed out that this wedding was the opposite of the usual, where the good stuff was served first and later, when people didn't notice, the cheaper, poorer vintage was poured. At this party, however, they had brought out the best possible wine long after the feast was underway.

Mary dimly grasped that the point of the episode was not the alcoholic content of the liquid served, nor when nor how it changed from H_2O into fermented grape juice. Furthermore, Mary understood that Jesus emphatically was not posing as a better-than-average trickster-showman, performing a clever sleight-of-hand stunt. Mary and the other guests that day comprehended that the changing of water into wine was a sign. They saw that the sign announced the new age that Jesus claimed to bring.

Later, they understood more fully what this sign meant. The episode pointed to the way in which Jesus supersedes all previous religious customs and institutions. He even replaces all that those stone jars, symbols of a rigid legalism and a tired busyness in religion, stood for. Jesus, they eventually learned, is enough. He takes the place of all that those jars or any other forms tried to do. Next to him, the purification ceremonies become pointless. Like the bubbly effervescence of the finest wine, his refreshing presence enlivens all the worn-out religious symbols and ceremonies. In him, there is life! Jesus, they understood, truly instituted a new age!

Around Nazareth, however, people began to mutter about Jesus, Mary noticed. When Jesus began to spend most of his time preaching in the more populated area near Capernaum, Mary felt relieved. At least she would not have to endure the jibes and comments of her fellow villagers about Jesus' preaching, she told herself.

Mary soon heard that Jesus had become a celebrity in Capernaum. She learned that huge crowds followed him everywhere, eager to hear his electrifying sermons. Mary felt deeply disquieted when she also learned that her son had reportedly rejected the rules of pious Jewish behavior. He was skipping the fasts and not strictly observing the Sabbath, Mary was told. Deeply grieved and upset, Mary asked herself where she had gone wrong.

The turning point came when the sensational news carried to Nazareth that Jesus had pronounced a paralytic forgiven. Everyone believed that illness was God's punishment. What right did Jesus have to forgive a paralyzed man, who obviously was getting what was coming to him from God? Jesus had gone too far, people said.

Furthermore, Mary learned that her son was hobnobbing with "undesirables." She wept inwardly when she heard that he ate with sinners and had even welcomed Levi, the notorious official who collected taxes on the fish at Capernaum, into his closest circle of associates.

What kind of kingdom was he inaugurating? Mary wondered. Jesus' new age seemed so unreligious to her. It didn't square at all with her understanding of the message from the divinely-sent announcer before she conceived. What did Jesus mean? Why was he acting so strangely?

Confused and hurt, Mary decided that she would intervene. She discussed the matter with her other sons, James, Joses, Jude and Simon, and convinced them that they would have to bring Jesus home. Jesus' notoriety was exposing them to the glare of publicity. It was time that Jesus returned with them to the obscurity of Nazareth and let the controversy subside. Mary, a good Jewish mother, thought to herself how she would look after him once she got him home again. She planned how she would cook his favorite dishes, and told herself that undoubtedly part of his problems had been due to his not eating properly. Some rest, some decent meals, and some attention would bring Jesus around in no time, Mary assured herself, and he could resume his mission for God by preaching on the Sabbaths in the Nazareth synagogue.

Mary and some of her other sons made the long trip by foot to Capernaum, a bustling fishing town on the shore of Galilee. They easily located Jesus—all they had to do was follow the crowds.

Mary was disturbed. She had heard that Jesus was receiving widespread attention, but had never imagined that he was attracting throngs like this.

Astonished, Mary watched her oldest son heal a pathetic case—a local minor character in the town who had stumbled around the streets for years making odd grunting noises because he was both blind and dumb. The most unsettling part, however, came when she heard Jesus excoriate the Jerusalem scribes and other religious authorities. Mary gasped. She heard words and a tone which cut and slashed like sword thrusts. Looking around her, she noticed the angry red faces, with the veins standing out and throbbing, the clenched jaws and the furious scowls of the Pharisees present. She shuddered, realizing that Jesus was incurring the enmity of the religious power structure. When someone whispered that Herod's agents were swarming everywhere, she became aware that Jesus' words were also stirring up the hostility of the Romans, too. It was no place for her boy to be, Mary fleetingly thought.

Stiffly refusing to enter the place where Jesus was speaking, Mary and Jesus' brothers remained outside. Instead of going inside, they sent word to Jesus that they wanted to talk to him.

Jesus stopped speaking when someone interrupted to tell him that his relatives were waiting outside. Jesus immediately knew that his mother and brothers were preparing a formal appeal to get him to return home. Stretching out his hands toward his listeners, he replied, "Here are my mother and my brothers! For whoever does the will of my Father in heaven is my brother, and sister, and mother" (Matthew 12:50).

Mary could not understand that her son's true relatives were those who joined him in obeying the Father's will. Real kinship, this possessive mother had to learn, rested not on blood ties or lineage, but on common obedience to God.

It was a painful scene. Mary's son was not behaving the way she wanted him to. She fretted. Why did this person who was flesh of her flesh seem to be such a contentious stranger?

Mary trudged back to Nazareth. As the conflict about Jesus mounted, she became more confused. She kept a dogged maternal devotion to Jesus because he was one of her own offspring, but she could not understand his program or his preaching. If only he would come home to Nazareth, marry a nice village girl, take up his trade again, raise a family, and be a respectable Jewish son, Mary wished.

Jesus did come to Nazareth one more time. The visit turned into a fiasco. On the Sabbath, he went to the synagogue. Mary beamed as he took the scroll. She wished that Joseph could see him now. She allowed herself the luxury of reminiscing. So many memories of Joseph and Jesus were associated with that little synagogue.

Unrolling the scroll to Isaiah (61:1,2) Jesus read the Hebrew words: "The Spirit of the Lord God is upon me, because the Lord has anointed me to bring good tidings to the afflicted; he has sent me . . . to proclaim liberty to the captives, and the opening of the prison . . . to proclaim the year of the Lord's favor. . . ." (See also Luke 4:18,19.)

Mary caught her breath. Would Jesus think that the passage referred to *him?* She noted that every person in the room waited tensely for his comments.

"Today," Jesus began, "this scripture has been fulfilled in your hearing" (Luke 4:21). He continued his sermon, pointing out that as God's spokesman, he—as many earlier prophets—had found no acceptance in Israel. Just as Elijah and Elisha, the greatest of God's men of old, had encountered faith among outsiders, so Jesus made clear that he would turn to others. Since the Jewish authorities rejected him, Jesus stated that he would bring God's new age to the poor, the captives, the blind, the oppressed, whether they were Jews or not!

Nazareth never forgot—or forgave—what they regarded as blasphemy by one of its sons that day. Rising out of their seats, shouting violently, the men in the synagogue stopped Jesus' sermon. The scene grew more unruly. Women screamed, and hurried the smaller children out of the building. Several men seized Jesus, angrily denouncing him.

Mary shook with terror. These were her neighbors and lifelong friends, she knew—and they were threatening to lynch her own son! She longed to protect her Jesus from harm. As the struggling, shouting mass of men surged out of the synagogue, Mary tried to plead with everyone. Middle-aged and stout, a woman and a widow, she realized that she was totally helpless. Powerless and grief-stricken, she stood in the street, watching the dust cloud which followed the angry crowd determined to push her son to his death by hurling him from a cliff. Her once-pretty face, now leathery and lined by years of bone-grinding toil and poverty, twitched as she fought to control her sorrow and fear.

Her daughters and some of her sons gently helped her back to her tiny hut, where she sat moaning. When James came in later, she expected to hear the worst. Although James reported that Jesus managed to get away safely, Mary immediately knew that Jesus would never again return home. She also knew that somehow, she would have to face the neighbors who had tried to kill her boy and had run him out of town. Mary felt so alone. It was as desolate as when she was pregnant with Jesus, when nobody had understood except Elizabeth and steady old Joseph. She ached for comfort. She found herself wishing that Joseph were still alive and could take her in his arms and hold her.

Mary bravely continued to live in Nazareth. Daily, she carried her water jar to the village well and tried to take part in the conversations with the other women. She kept house as usual for the children still at home, rising at dawn to start the fire and plodding through the wearisome round of peasant-wife's work until sundown and the final trip to the village well. She thought constantly of Jesus. She listened intently to every scrap of news or rumor about him which anybody carried up to Nazareth from the outside world. Perplexed but still the protective mother, Mary entertained thoughts of going to Capernaum again. She shrewdly guessed that his time was growing short. Piecing together the snippets of intelligence about Jesus which reached Nazareth, Mary deduced that he planned to head to Jerusalem, the capital, for a final mighty effort to convince the religious authorities of his mission to Israel.

Mary determined to spend Passover in Jerusalem herself, to join Jesus in the holy city. When she urged some of her other sons to go with her, however, she found that they had already had all the publicity and embarrassment as members of Jesus' family that they wanted. Even James, as devout a young man as she had ever seen, refused to go to Jerusalem for Passover that year. She learned, to her sorrow, that her other children continued to smart from the neighbors' comments about their famous brother.

Mary linked up with one of the many pilgrim groups traveling south for the high holy days in Jerusalem. Although she had made the three-day journey before, she had never felt so tired at the end of each day. The years were beginning to exact their toll on her strength.

When she arrived at Jerusalem, she had never encountered such feverish excitement or tension. Everyone buzzed with rumors, she discovered, and most of these rumors had to do with Jesus. Mary heard some state that he was the Messiah, and would enter the city to liberate it from the Romans and set up a new kingdom like King David's. The Messiah! The Deliverer! Mary had long harbored secret suspicions that her son would be the Promised One to Israel, but of course, had never told anyone, even in her own family.

When Mary saw Jesus come into Jerusalem amidst a royal welcome, she felt a surge of excitement and pride. However, when she heard about his exploits in the temple, driving out the animal peddlers and coin changers, she wondered what kind of a Messiah he meant to be. She knew that Jesus was not following the script for a Messiah. Everybody expected the Messiah to move against the Romans, not against the temple system and the religious authorities. Mary intuitively grasped that her son was in deep trouble.

So many people seemed to be swirling around Jesus that Mary could not get near to speak to him in private. Nighttimes, when she thought she might have a word with him to plead with him to be careful, she could not find him. Mary sensed that with each hour pressures seemed to be stepped up to silence Jesus. It all seemed so bewildering, so terrifying to Mary.

Nobody paid much attention to the white-haired little old lady with the stooped shoulders and the lined face outside Pilate's hall. Her calloused hands, rough, black dress and north-country accent marked her as a typical woman from the villages. No one suspected that this peasant widow mingling with the shoving, shouting crowds was the mother of the man on trial for his life inside.

Mary had spent so many sleepless nights during the past week that she did not care that no one recognized her. In fact, she had even resigned herself to not being able to speak to Jesus. All she hoped to do was to be near her son. In her weariness, she prayed for him. Unable to understand him or the events carrying him to his trial before the Romans, she simply planned to stay as close to him as she could.

"Crucify him! Crucify him!" The baying of the mob for her son's life made Mary wince. Suddenly, she caught a glimpse of him, as the squad of soldiers manhandled him roughly through the crowd. She could tell that Jesus was exhausted. And his back, she noted with horror, carried long, raw bloody stripes from a severe flogging. Mary longed to apply soothing ointment to the wounds.

The execution squad dragged Jesus through the narrow streets at the head of a screaming mob. Mary, caught up in the slipstream, found herself following the procession.

Numbly, Mary halted at the foot of Golgotha, the execution hill outside the city gates. She knew well what crucifixion meant for her son and herself. Execution on a cross meant an insidiously inhumane form of lingering and torturous death. Moreover, Mary, as a pious Jew, had been raised to understand that death on a cross was the most scandalously disgraceful way of dying for any Jew. Mary, accepting the fact that she would be shamed for the rest of her life as the mother of a crucified criminal and outcast, remained to be with her son as he died.

She flinched and turned her head as the executioners nailed the spikes through her son's hands. Those hands, Mary remembered, were once tiny and chubby and pink. She mused that those hands, now crippled and bloody, had once as baby hands clutched her finger held over his cradle. Mary recalled how his hands had clung to her skirt to steady himself when he had learned to walk, had held tightly around her neck when she had picked him up when he had fallen and had cried. Mary had noticed his hands so quickly had developed into man's hands, broad, powerful—a workingman's hands like Joseph's, with scratches and callouses on the palms. And now. . . .

She found her reverie interrupted by groans of pain. Looking up, Mary heard her son gasp, "I'm thirsty." She wanted to moisten his dry lips, but the soldiers made it clear that no one was to interfere. Mary could only stand helplessly, watching her son gasp in agony to keep on breathing, as his chest and diaphragm muscles, stretched into unnatural position by supporting his weight on the cross, struggled to inflate and deflate his lungs. Too young to die so horribly, she thought, and too good to die so disgracefully. Mary felt crushed with grief.

All those secrets about his kingship stored up for so many years, Mary thought, were to be ended absurdly with a hammer and some nails and two planks, the same tools and materials her Joseph and Jesus had so often worked with. A carpenter done in with the articles of the carpenter's trade seemed to her to add an ironic touch. And dying on a cross was not the way a Messiah concluded his career.

The crowds thinned. A long, boring wait for a victim to die did not entice people wanting action and drama. The soldiers on duty wearily tossed dice to while away the time and divide the victims' effects. Some bystanders tried to liven up the afternoon by taunting the gasping, writhing victims.

In her loneliness, Mary had not paid any attention to any others by the cross. She had not noticed that one of the Twelve also stood grieving.

The one disciple present was John. He, in turn, had been so preoccupied with his own sorrow that he had ignored others, including Mary. Although he had been more of a brother to Jesus than Jesus' own brothers, he had failed to observe his best friend's mother. John, isolated by watching the dying of his closest friend, felt that life was over for him, too.

In spite of his pain and dizziness, Jesus recognized two of the figures standing on the edge of the clearing as the two who had remained with him until the very end. Grimly fighting to keep from lapsing into unconsciousness and struggling to speak, Jesus spoke to Mary and John, the two who were more devoted to him than any others.

"Woman, here is your son," he croaked to Mary. "Here is your mother," he gasped to John (John 19:26, 27 TEV).

He told Mary to "adopt" John as her own, and instructed John to take Jesus' place as her son. Jesus gave Mary to John, and John to Mary, telling each to look after the other.

To keep the two from becoming totally absorbed in personal sorrow, Jesus commended them to each other's care. Each, he perceived, needed strength and love. And each would get it from the other.

Mary and John learned that Jesus' way of handling grief is to minister to others. Instead of weeping and brooding in solitude, they each found the healing which comes from relating to others. They understood that they were liberated from bondage to self-pity. They were no longer enslaved by sadness. At the cross, they discovered, Jesus liberated them.

Only in the light of the Resurrection, however, did Mary begin to understand that the child born to her truly was the "Son of the Most High" exactly as the Messenger had promised. Mary had been mystified during all of Jesus' career because he had not followed the pattern of the Messiah which she and everyone had expected. Although Mary in a sense represented all the best in Jewish womanhood, with a spiritual sensitivity no other had, and although Mary remained faithful to God, with an unshakeable loyalty to tradition, Mary had felt confused by Jesus' words and acts. She had painstakingly raised her boy by the best religious standards. She was dismayed to think, that in the name of God, Jesus was repudiating many of those same standards. It took the Resurrection to dissolve her doubts and anxiety.

Mary came to exemplify the woman truly liberated—freed to live, freed to be a person, freed to care. God's tremendous act of suffering love through the cross and Resurrection of her son, Mary learned, sets free every woman.

Not unsurprisingly, Mary joyfully associated herself with that band of believers in the Risen Jesus which threw away all the old ideas about woman's "place" and woman's "role." Mary and those who had been convened by the Resurrected Christ ceased to think of themselves as slaves of custom. As liberated persons, they most frequently called themselves *slaves* of Christ!

"All these [referring to Jesus' disciple band] with one accord devoted themselves to prayer, together with the women and Mary the mother of Jesus, and with his brothers" (Acts 1:14), the early church record informs us. *Together with the women,* meaning that the Resurrection of Jesus Christ ignited the first and most lasting Women's Lib movement in the world. No second-class citizenship for females here. No prayers of thanks to a God "Who has not made me a woman" in this group.

As the first woman to be mentioned by name in the roll of those who gathered in the Upper Room after the Ascension, Mary is the prototype of woman as person rather than function. Mary, the truly liberated woman, is acceptable, and accepted and accepting.

The gospel, women (and men, too!) continue to discover, still is the most dynamically liberating force. It is still news of One who as Liberator came "to proclaim release to the captives . . . to set at liberty those who are oppressed" (Luke 4:18).

THE WIDOW
(Anna)

She had installed herself in the temple courtyard for so many years that she had become a semiofficial fixture. Without intending to become a tourist sight, she nevertheless received stares from visitors looking for local color.

Wizened, wheezy, and toothless, like a prehistoric mummy which breathed, the ancient woman sat in what had by years' habit become known as "Anna's station," a location she chose for herself on the main thoroughfare in the temple precincts.

In an era when a woman was old at thirty, and on borrowed time after forty, Anna at eighty-four appeared almost timeless. Records were scanty and ambiguous, but old-timers reported that Anna had been married as a young maiden, but widowed after only seven years with her husband. Since her husband's death, she had lived alone, and all her hours during all the years of her long widowhood had been spent in the temple area.

In time, the title, *Prophetess,* had been conferred by common agreement out of respect for her spiritual perceptivity. Although some of the younger, with-it crowd did not hold her in highest veneration, thinking people listened to Anna's keen insights on God and His intentions for His people in current times.

The very word *Prophetess* or *Prophet* means "one who speaks for God" and a prophetess's words carried clout. The title, given sparingly to women, had been borne by such spiritual giantesses as Deborah, Huldah, Miriam, Noadiah and Isaiah's wife—all believed to be divinely inspired to be able to reveal God's will to others. When Prophetess Anna spoke, the devout paid her close heed.

Anna, however, said little. Day after day, year in and year out, she unobtrusively shuffled to her regular place in the temple yard. She observed every time for worship. Although the normal days for fasting were Mondays and Thursdays, Anna frequently fasted on other occasions. Even on nonfast days, she subsisted on a few handfuls of food, taken between her evening prayers. Most of her waking hours, in fact, were devoted to praying and worshiping. After dark, she slowly padded to a protected portico, unrolled a worn mat, wrapped an ancient shawl around her wizened body, mumbled her last words of praise to God for the day's goodness, and stretched out for sleep. She always woke before daylight.

Anna, named for Hannah, Samuel's mother (1 Samuel 1:2) sometimes reflected on the fact that her name derived from the Hebrew word, *grace*. God's grace, Hannah steadfastly believed, overflowed her life. Her prayers and meditations, never morose or world-weary, reflected the joy and hope of a woman who faced the future on tiptoes. Her worship acts were not mechanical, merit-earning efforts to get God's approval. Rather, whether she fasted or feasted, she did everything in grateful response to His grace.

After eighty-four years of living, Anna did not romanticize life. Personal sorrow and loneliness had sharpened her sense of the tragedy in human existence.

Whenever Anna recalled her ancestry, she felt this tragic sense intensified. Anna, descendant from a distinguished family, could trace her lineage to the tribe of Asher, the clan of Jacob's eighth son, and one of the largest when the tribes left Egypt in Moses' time. Imbued with the traditions of the Asherites, Anna knew that the daughters of the tribe of Asher were the only ones celebrated for their beauty, and the only women fitted to be married to high priests or a king. Anna, with sorrow, also knew that her tribe had declined, and had suffered the ignominy of being one of the ten tribes carried off in the Assyrian invasion some seven hundred years earlier. Although individual stragglers from her tribe such as her own ancestors had remembered their heritage, and returned from captivity, Anna nonetheless brooded on how most of her tribe, the large and once-proud people of Asher were still in exile.

Not only were her own kinfolk apparently hopelessly homeless; the future of Jerusalem and Judea was in doubt. Anna as a prophetess grasped what few others (except later, Jesus) understood: her country was on a collision course with disaster. The social, moral and political crisis in Jerusalem, Anna sensed, was so profound that the nation could not survive. She longed deeply for one to redeem Israel, to awaken its people to their destiny as God's own.

It was only Anna's tenacious sense of trust in God's grace which kept her from succumbing to despair.

Anna waited. For decades, she looked for "the redemption of Jerusalem" (Luke 2:38).

Anna, certain that God would vindicate her waiting, continued to pray and fast and worship. Her once-beautiful Asherite face had shriveled with age. Her eyes, the fluid caked on the edges, had filmed over with cataracts. Like a fragile, dried husk, her octogenarian body looked so shrunken and light that a breeze would push it over. It almost seemed as if her faded black dress kept her propped up. Friends sometimes advised her not to go to the temple to worship, but to pray in a more comfortable setting. In spite of the blustery winds swirling from the Judean hills through the broad temple yards, Anna faithfully maintained her temple discipline of regular worship and waiting, waiting and praying, fasting and waiting, waiting and waiting.

Few people that day took notice of the Jewish man and his young wife from the country with the small baby. Hundreds of pious peasant couples, all near the margin of poverty, all journeying to Jerusalem at great personal cost, passed through the great courtyard of the temple each day. Many carried babies. Because the Jewish Law required parents to present the first child to the Lord at the Jerusalem temple, it was a common sight for young fathers and mothers carrying infants to be in the crowds which usually bustled about the temple precincts. Anna, in her sixty years of people-watching and praying in the temple, had seen countless couples bearing their youngsters, pushing through the throngs to offer their sacrifices.

The Jewish man from the country, Joseph, the Nazareth carpenter, and his tired young wife, Mary, were walking through the wide area inside the walled-off temple grounds. They too, had a baby—their first child, a son, named Jesus. Joseph and Mary were too intent on locating the place where they were to present the child and sacrifice a pigeon as their offering, to notice Anna, or another ancient, well-known figure in Jerusalem named Simeon.

Simeon, led by the Spirit, detected that the infant Jesus was God's instrument of saving Israel. The old man joyfully took the baby in his arms and praised God. Blessing Mary and Joseph, Simeon handed the baby back to them. "Behold," he told Mary, "this child is set for the fall and rising of many in Israel . . ." (2:34).

At that moment, Anna hobbled up and entered the scene. Her faith and patience were rewarded. She saw in the child Jesus the fulfillment of God's promise to His people. Anna's long wait was over! In the midst of the tears and tragedy of life, Anna understood that in the person of Jesus, God brought redemption to Israel.

Every woman and every man plays the waiting game. Everyone is waiting for something—to grow up, to get a driver's license, to get away from home, to finish school, to get married, to have the baby, to buy the new house, to get the big promotion, to get the children through school, to get a little laid aside, to retire, to die. At the same time, everyone senses that he or she is waiting for something more—or is it Someone?

Samuel Beckett's play, *Waiting for Godot*, portrays two penniless, smelly tramps waiting in a barren countryside for a third party named Godot. Godot does not show up. Periodically, there are announcements that Godot will soon make an appearance, but he never comes in view. Meanwhile, the two characters on stage become intolerably bored and cranky. They try to work up a sense of companionship, but find little likeable in each other. They cannot even entertain each other, but weary each other with their poses. The play's dialogue meanders pointlessly, reflecting the longing of the two tramps for a glimpse of Godot who never comes, or ever will. The central noncharacter in the play, of course, is Godot, and Beckett, choosing the diminutive for "God," would have us understand that God never will put in an appearance. Man's absurd plight, according to Beckett, is that he persists in waiting for God, the God who never comes and never will.

The waiting game is over. God has put in an appearance—a very *personal* appearance—in the form of Mary's baby. God has come on to the stage of time and space, at a specific date and place.

Anna understood this. After encountering Jesus, her waiting days were over. The marvelous news that day in the temple court was that God had come! She knew that she was freed from having to wait. Everything in her eighty-four years had been leading up to that stupendous meeting.

Tennessee Williams' *The Milk Train Doesn't Stop Here Anymore* depicts vulgar, aging, rich-girl loudmouth, Flora Goforth, who, in spite of her three villas in Italy and jet-set pals, begins to ponder her old age and demise. Waiting for death, Flora realizes faintly that she may also be waiting for the Someone. "Bring God to me!" she whines. "How do you do it, whistle, ring a bell for Him?"

Out of the emptiness of waiting for God-knows-who, without our signals or efforts, God has chosen to disclose Himself through Jesus. God is known through God alone. Our knowledge of Him will always be second-hand until and except as we are confronted by Him as He has decided to reveal Himself. And it is through the person of Mary's baby that God, oddly enough, has seen fit to introduce Himself in His personal way.

Anna, learning this, "spoke of him to all who were looking for the redemption of Israel" (2:38). The tense of the verb, *spoke*, means that she kept speaking and speaking of Jesus, over and over again, to everyone who would listen.

And whether she lived another day, another year or another eighty-four, Anna now knew that the gospel's show-and-tell life was the purpose of living.

And yours?

Like Aunt Catherine in Paddy Chayefsky's *Marty?* Not knowing what or whom she is waiting for, and dreading her old age, she grumbles, "It's gonna happen to you. Mark it well. These terrible years. I'm afraid to look inna mirror. I'm afraid I'm gonna see an old lady with white hair, like the old ladies inna park, little bundles inna black shawl, waiting for the coffin. I'm fifty-six years old. What am I gonna do with myself? I have strength in my hands. I wanna cook. I wanna clean. I wanna make dinner for my children. I wanna be of use to somebody. Am I an old dog to lie in fronta the fire till my eyes close? These are terrible years, Theresa! Terrible years!"

Anna would have disagreed. Terrible years? Never! Instead, her sentiments would have agreed with the late Angus Dun, who once said, "I have learned that human existence is essentially tragic. It is the love of God, disclosed and enacted in Christ, that redeems the human tragedy and makes it tolerable. No, more than tolerable, wonderful!"

It's worth waiting eighty-four years, if necessary, to learn this Good News which makes the human tragedy wonderful!

THE SUPERMOM
(Salome)

Nothing was too good for her boys. Protective and ambitious for James and John, her two sons, Salome went to any lengths to make sure they got the best. And for Salome, "the best" even included the choice seats beside the throne in God's Kingdom.

While still a girl, she had married a burly fisherman named Zebedee. Salome and Zebedee settled in one of the fishing villages which ringed the tempestuous lake called the Sea of Galilee.

Salome quickly adjusted to the rugged existence. Each evening after cooking a big meal and packing a lunch for her man, she watched him push out in the boat to throw his nets all night. At dawn the following morning, she met him on the beach as he and his mates returned with the night's catch.

Often, Salome had to help drag in the heavy nets. She did not complain, however; heavy nets meant a good catch, and money to pay the bills. As soon as the nets were hauled into the shallow water, Salome and the others started to separate the fish, heaving the keepers on shore and tossing the smaller or inedible ones back in the lake. It was tiring work, but Salome worked energetically.

Next, everyone hurried to clean the catch. It was imperative to gut, split and lay out the fish on the drying racks immediately before the decay process started. Salome and the other fishwives worked quickly and efficiently. Salome enjoyed the rough banter.

When the filets of fish were finally lying on the racks to dry in the hot sun, Salome, weary and reeking of fish odors, hurried back to her hut to prepare a meal. She knew that Zebedee, hungry from heaving nets and dragging lines all night and mending equipment after landing at dawn, would be ravenously hungry.

While Zebedee slept, Salome washed, mended, pounded the grain to make the barley flour for their bread, gathered greens for stews and performed the thousand and one items of toil which fell to a Palestinian housewife.

As soon as their two sons were strong enough to stay awake all night and tug in nets, Salome allowed them to join Zebedee. Extra hands meant extra income, and in their lean budget, every denarius counted. Salome proudly watched James and John grow into robust lads.

Although living in peasant poverty, Salome and Zebedee and their boys devoutly attended worship each Sabbath. They conscientiously tried to be good Jews. Money, however, was too scarce to purchase the extra complete set of dishes to observe all the ceremonial cleanliness required of orthodox believers. Salome sometimes resented being labeled one of the "people of the land," the opprobrious term of the strict Jewish scribes for those who did not scrupulously observe the Law. Nonetheless, she dutifully taught James and John their prayers.

On holidays, Salome and her family sometimes journeyed up the winding mountain road to Nazareth, where her sister, Mary, and her husband, Joseph the carpenter, lived. Other times, Salome and Zebedee welcomed their Nazareth relatives to their seaside home. Salome noticed that the children, led by Jesus, Mary and Joseph's eldest, enjoyed playing together.

Existence in the fishing village depended upon the fluctuating catches, upon the weather, upon the winds, upon the currents, upon the seasons, upon the stamina of the fishermen, upon the condition of the boats, nets and equipment, upon the prices paid for dried fish—upon so many variables. A slight drop in the wholesale price, or several nights without a good catch, and the fishwives went hungry to feed their menfolk. Tempers sometimes grew short. Fights occasionally broke out.

The Sea of Galilee, actually a lake only thirteen miles by seven, is situated in a deep pocket below sea level. Directly to the north tower the snow-capped ranges of Lebanon, beginning with Mt. Hermon. The area is a natural magnet for intense storm systems, making the Sea of Galilee one of the most treacherous and unpredictable bodies of water in the world. In ten minutes, the surface can change from a tranquil pond into a surging maelstrom.

Salome and most of the fisherfolk around Galilee seemed to acquire the lake's characteristics. Usually calm and pleasant, Salome and her sons could blow up into a squall with little warning or provocation. Salome's sons, in fact, picked up such a reputation for stormy combativeness that they were nicknamed "Sons of Thunder." Sometimes shrill and pushy, Salome easily revealed her status as a fishwife.

Salome doted on her two sons. She aggressively urged them on in everything they did. Perhaps compensating for her own sense of insecurity, she taught them not to allow themselves to be pushed around. Life was like the fishmarket, Salome taught them; one had to scramble and shove to get the best place. The rewards went to those with the biggest catch in the front of the line.

Salome knew that she often got bumped aside in the struggle to be first.

For another thing, the daily round of hardscrabbling work was in actuality a brutal contest between Salome and the chores. Sometimes Salome won —barely—and the challenge of the list of tasks was met—for that day. Usually the work won, and Salome, defeated and depressed, fell on her sleeping mat in exhaustion. It often seemed that her many jobs, constantly battling her wits and energies and waking hours, were meant to crush her because she was a woman.

Moreover, it seemed that as a woman, she was always being elbowed aside in life simply because she was a woman in what was unquestionably a male-dominated world. Although Salome could not articulate the hostilities she felt because she was discriminated against as a woman, she nonetheless felt the deep, lasting burn on her psyche. The prejudice against women in the world sharpened her flinty competitiveness. Salome met the antifeminist roadblocks in her life by becoming fiercely ambitious for her two sons. Although the world might have pushed her around as a woman, Salome was grimly determined that her two sons would be given preeminence. Compensating for her own second-class status, she pressed for first-class treatment for James and John. Salome planned a sort of liberation from her degrading role of fishwife by vicariously living through her children's success.

The syndrome is still present, as any school official or Little League coach will testify!

And our society—Women's Lib notwithstanding—still degrades women. Listen to some rock lyrics. As the titles of some songs contemptuously suggest, a woman is a "Stupid Girl" expected to "Light My Fire" sexually, always kept "Under My Thumb" although she may "Live with Me," but always a "Honky Tonk Woman" existing only to give me "Satisfaction," then discarded like "Yesterday's Papers."

Plastic plaything, disposable object? Our culture still says, *Yes, a woman is a commodity.* Although some songs portray women either as insatiable, sex-crazed animals or all-American emasculators, in the end they all wind up in a servile role, existing only to enhance the lives of males. As one verse by the Rolling Stones arrogantly shrills, *Who wants yesterday's papers,*

Who wants yesterday's girl? (who once used is presumably good only for wrapping garbage).

In a society which still idealized woman as a dehumanized, dependent dummy, it is inevitable that women should revolt. "Quentin, I am not a praise machine! I am not a blur, and I am not your mother! I am a separate person!" Louise snaps in *After the Fall*, Arthur Miller's play.

In many ways, Salome is a prototype for today's Supermom. Driving and restless, Supermom is unwilling to accept the stereotype of woman being submissive, stupid, or silly. Supermom realizes that she herself may never get out of the back seat, but she is determined that her kids will hold the wheel.

When, a few years later, her nephew Jesus appeared healing and preaching, Salome encouraged her sons, James and John, to join him. It gave Salome satisfaction to see her two strong sons among Jesus' friends. People spoke admiringly of Jesus in those days, and Salome felt that nice things said about Jesus were also nice things about her sons, and therefore nice things about her.

Salome talked almost incessantly with the other fishwives and villagers about her sons. When she heard that Jesus had selected James and John to join his inner circle of Twelve, Salome was elated. Although it meant considerable financial hardship because they would not be joining Zebedee on the boat, Salome cheerfully sacrificed a large portion of the family income for the publicity and prominence given her two boys.

She listened eagerly for every report of James and John and the others in Jesus' disciple group. Whenever possible, she trudged to Capernaum, the center of Jesus' Galilee operations for a time. She seldom was able to spend time alone with James and John, but she always left them some pickled fish and a few fresh barley loaves as a mother's expression of love and devotion. Always the Mom, Salome fussed because her boys did not seem to be getting enough rest. Jesus, Salome noticed, had become so phenomenally popular that the crowds hounded him and his close associates every waking hour.

Jesus, Salome observed proudly, leaned on her two sons. Along with Simon Peter, another rough-handed Galilean fisherman, her sons were part of the inner circle of Jesus' followers. "Peter, James and John," people chimed, repeating the names of the trio of leaders in Jesus' band, almost as if they were reciting a popular verse. Salome beamed. The only thing which could have increased her pride would have been to hear the saying run, "James, John, and Peter," putting her sons' names first.

Salome became anxious for her sons' safety, however, when she heard rumors that both Herod, the wily, cruel ruler of Galilee, and the religious leaders had begun to spy on Jesus. Jesus' criticisms of the leadership in the country, Salome shrewdly suspected, were not well received in high places.

Several times, Salome wondered whether her rabbi nephew was not up to something more than religious reform. So many of his speeches seemed to have political overtones. Salome anxiously considered at times that Jesus and her sons might be hatching a revolt against the Romans. She shuddered. How well she knew the record of such attempts to throw out the Romans in the past. She could never forget seeing the rows of dead and dying participants in past revolts. Each victim, Salome remembered, had been suspended gruesomely by the hands, which had been nailed to beams resting on the tops of upright poles.

Salome also knew that Galilee had the reputation of being the spawning ground for rebellion. Clandestine societies were constantly organizing. Guerilla groups were always planning raids. Furtive men were known to be hiding in mountain caves to escape Roman army patrols. Were James and John getting mixed up with one of these movements?

In spite of assurances from some of her friends that Jesus planned no insurrection, Salome was not convinced. Jesus' rhetoric perplexed her. What did he mean when he talked about "the Kingdom of God," and "I have not come to bring peace but a sword?" (Matthew 10:34).

And if Jesus were a good Jewish rabbi, Salome asked herself, why did he persistently take such a casual attitude toward the Law? She had heard that a deputation of scribes and Pharisees had come all the way from Jerusalem to take Jesus and his disciples to task for their laxness, demanding, "Why do your disciples transgress the tradition of the elders? For they do not wash their hands when they eat" (Matthew 15:2). That stung Salome. She had raised her sons to be devout hand-washing Jews. She did not like them being accused of being transgressors or irreligious. Was Jesus leading them astray from the true faith? she worried.

Salome watched carefully what was happening to Jesus and her sons. Her shrewd fishwife's insights informed her that a crisis was brewing. At the same time, she heard the rumors whisking through Galilee that some said that Jesus was the Messiah.

Her own nephew, the Messiah! Salome's pulse quickened at the thought. She remembered that she had always thought that Mary's oldest boy was, well, *different*. Imagine, Jesus, the Promised One, Israel's Deliverer! she thought.

Dimly, she began to comprehend some of Jesus' cryptic comments about his "Kingdom." The Messianic Kingdom, God's new age, of course! She understood better why he had spoken the way he had.

As a Galilean peasant woman, Salome had a limited vision of the Kingdom. Simplistically, she assumed (as most others did) that it involved marching into Jerusalem, kicking out the Romans, reinstituting a monarchy like David's and living happily ever after.

Although Jesus consistently repudiated this kind of a kingdom, Salome and most others did not really hear him. They did not want to hear of any type of kingdom except the one set up by the Strongman on the Charger who would humble the hated Romans.

Salome cunningly began to plan. If, as so many said, Jesus were the Messiah, and if he would advance to Jerusalem to set up his rule, as the Messiah must, she reasoned that Jesus would need chief lieutenants. And if he needed lieutenants, what better ones than James and John, her sons?

Furthermore, Salome understood the labyrinthine ways of politics in the Middle East. It took pull, she perceived, to get anywhere. Only those with friends in the right place, those who knew someone who could speak a word here or put a few coins there, moved up to key jobs. Bribes, payoffs, under-the-table deals and nepotism were all names of the game.

Salome knew she would never have cash to promote her sons. She suddenly realized that she had even better leverage. She was the aunt of the Messiah! She was willing to use her family relationship to advance her sons' interests. How could Jesus turn down a request to install her James and John in the places of honor? That was the way the System operated.

Salome consulted with James and John on the best way to approach Jesus. With their connivance, Salome took it upon herself to go to him herself and ask for a personal favor.

Ironically, the moment Salome chose to present her demand that Jesus install her sons as co-vice-presidents of the Kingdom came immediately after he had talked to his disciples about his coming sacrifice.

"Behold, we are going up to Jerusalem," Jesus soberly had warned James and John and the others of the Twelve; "and the Son of man will be delivered to the chief priests and scribes, and they will condemn him to death, and deliver him to the Gentiles to be mocked and scourged and crucified, and he will be raised on the third day" (Matthew 20:18, 19).

This was the third time Jesus had explicitly told the disciples that he would inaugurate his Kingdom by dying painfully and disgracefully for others. His type of Kingdom, Jesus made clear, entailed serving others and suffering for others. Self-advancement? There was simply no place for personal promotion. Caring for others was what counted.

Salome approached and interrupted. She must speak to Jesus about an important personal request. She knelt down in a suppliant position. Her tone and her words became emotional. Salome, her children's interest foremost, blinked back tears. She pleaded, "Command that these two sons of mine may sit, one at your right hand and one at your left, in your kingdom" (20:21).

It is hard to turn down a request from a close relative, especially when presented so imploringly. Jesus, however, was totally uninterested in passing around earthly honors or assigning places of glory in the heavenly Kingdom.

"You do not know what you are asking," he answered slowly. The throne and suffering go together. "Are you able to drink the cup that I am to drink?" he quietly asked (20:22).

James and John, who have been waiting nearby in anticipation of being named Number One and Number Two in the Kingdom, promptly chirped, "We are able."

Jesus sighed. He realized that Salome and her sons, his closest associates and his own relatives, had completely misconstrued his message. Patiently, he said, in effect, I don't mind allowing you to join in my sufferings. But sitting on the right hand and the left is another matter altogether and not simply a matter of personal favors. You see, in my Kingdom, favoritism has no place.

Hearing the grumbling among the other disciples who had just learned of Salome's scheme, Jesus called the entire group around him. "You know that the rulers of the Gentiles lord it over them," he stated bluntly, "and their great men exercise authority over them. It shall not be so among you; but whoever would be great among you must be your servant, and whoever would be first among you must be your slave." Jesus paused. Looking each man in the eye, he slowly drilled home the meaning of his life and coming death:

". . . the Son of man came not to be served but to serve, and to give his life as a ransom for many" (20:25–28).

Salome listened, but she did not understand. She still entertained selfish ambitions.

Every woman and every man puts together secret schemes of self-promotion. It is part of the human illness.

The woman Tarpeia, who betrayed Rome, ambitiously demanded as her reward "the things" the soldiers wear on their left arms. In addition to the soldiers' golden bracelets which she coveted, she found herself receiving their shields which they also carried on their left arms. She tried to snatch the bracelets, but was covered by such a heap of heavy shields that she was crushed to death.

Our selfish ambition can—and will—crush us.

We may nod agreement to this truism, but we really do not believe that it applies to us. We know how to operate. We're too smart to get crushed. If there is any threat of a crunch, we insist to ourselves that a little more know-how will save us. Not until it is too late do we learn that we need not data but deliverance, not schemes but salvation.

Not until the Cross and Resurrection was Salome liberated from her greedy aspirations and petty conniving.

She watched the execution, putting her head in her hands as Jesus died as he had predicted. She learned that Jesus was certainly not the triumphant king which she had expected him to be.

Only the Risen Lord untied her from her obsessive, presumptuous drives to advance herself through advancing her sons. The Resurrected Christ allowed her to be Salome and liberated her from trying to be Supermom.

Significantly, Salome's sons also were liberated by the Living One from their overweening fascination with Being Important. James became the first of the Twelve to be martyred (about A.D. 44 by Herod Agrippa) and traditions are unanimous that John also died for his faith.

Salome wept, but she had the satisfaction of knowing that each of her sons won the kind of preeminence which Jesus urged, namely, "to give his life as a ransom for many." What better ambition than to sacrifice for others?

THE CALL GIRL
(Woman Who Was a Sinner)

To everyone in Capernaum she was known as a whore. The camel drivers and fishermen regarded her as a pornographic plaything. The women resented and feared her. The rabbis and Pharisees anathematized her.

Luke, usually a meticulous record-keeper, does not mention her name. In spite of longstanding notions, she should not be identified with either Mary Magdalene or Mary of Bethany. There is not a shred of evidence in the New Testament to link her with any known personality. Luke, in fact, goes out of his way to conceal her identity in his gospel account (Luke 7). With his crisp physician's description, he states simply that she was "a woman of the city who was a sinner" (Luke 7:37).

Anonymous she may be, but from a general knowledge of prostitutes we can get a fairly good profile of her personality.

Every harlot studied feels alienated from society. Popular lore notwithstanding, in every known culture, a prostitute suffers a loss of social standing. Usually, she is condemned.

Girls turning to prostitution always have a personality problem. Selling their bodies for a man's pleasure is a symptom of deeper problems. Economic considerations do not explain why girls degrade themselves by peddling sex. And, contrary to popular opinion, all prostitutes feel that they work hard at their trade, and never feel that they work for pleasure. Moreover, psychiatric interviews reveal that such women are seldom sensuous, but actually tend to be sexually frigid.

How do they get that way? What drives girls toward prostitution? Psychoanalysts report that nearly all prostitutes have broken away from home and, beneath a surface of rebellious independence, feel deep hostilities toward their mothers and profound disappointment toward their fathers.

Severe loss of mother love caused these girls to turn to their fathers for affection, psychoanalytic reports state.

The girls, however, found that their fathers failed to give them the emotional support they needed. Deprived of love and security as children, they lived in a state of stunted growth, emotionally speaking, searching as grown women for the identity and warmth they had not received as little girls.

In the opinion of some analysts, the girls eventually fell to self-abasement as a way of hurting their parents. Prostitutes, in actuality, are trying to bring revenge on their fathers.

Every harlot interviewed reveals unconscious hostilities toward males. Avenging herself on all men by showing that the sex act—so important to him—means little or nothing to her, she consciously or unconsciously humiliates all men by having sexual relations with any and all.

The union of whore and client is a sado-masochistic relationship of debasement. Both are expressing aggression and hostility. The encounter is brief and incognito between pseudopersons. There is an absence of affection. While there is a brief physical closeness, there is no closeness of persons. Pathetically immature, both harlot and customer find it too threatening to accept a permanent bond. Even the money changing hands, according to reports of depth interviews by experts, is a symbol of mutual contempt.

Few prostitutes save their money or spend it wisely, but usually lavish it on costly trinkets they don't need or use, or splurge it on their men.

Deceit becomes part of the pathology of prostitution. A harlot will seldom tell the truth about herself, authorities report.

Untruthful and spiteful, all B-girls, call girls, prostitutes, and streetwalkers tend to transfer their guilt feelings to their customers. The girls rationalize that they are earning their pay while the customer is behaving deceitfully or immorally. Lying is part of the protective mechanism.

The whore in Capernaum—although nameless—fell into the dismal personality pattern of all prostitutes. In response to loneliness and rejection as a little girl, she succumbed to an extreme form of self-loathing. She became so antisocial that she had a desire to turn all men into swine.

Bawdy and coarse, she cheapened herself and everyone she took on as a customer for the evening. In turn, passed around like a smutty joke among the rowdies and misfits, she sank so low in the community's respect that she was called simply "a sinner."

"A Sinner." The word in Greek *(hamartolos)* means that she was obsessed with vice. Not just a bit naughty, but totally soaked in evil and dripping with a sordid past.

No wonder Jesus was accused of impropriety by befriending this woman. No respectable person wanted to taint himself by any association with this disgusting character. Reputations, after all, can be so easily besmirched.

Jesus, however, repeatedly stated, "I came not to call the righteous, but sinners" (Matthew 9:13). "The Son of man came to seek and to save the lost" (Luke 19:10). "Those who are well have no need of a physician, but those who are sick" (Matthew 9:12). "There will be more joy in heaven over one sinner who repents than over ninety-nine righteous persons who need no repentance" (Luke 15:7). And his actions backed his words.

He even convinced the whore in Capernaum.

The notorious local character, snickered at by the roughnecks from the boats and caravans, spat at by the housewives, bought and used by every drunken mule driver with a few spare coins, believed Jesus! This woman, who despised all men, had never encountered anyone like him! For the first time since she could remember, she met a man who did not try either to buy her or berate her.

Incredibly, she was convinced that Jesus represented God. God's judgment, to be sure, she had long sensed. Jesus' presence did not minimize that awareness of how disappointing her life was to her, to him, and to God. At the same time, she knew that Jesus took her seriously. So seriously, that he conveyed compassion yet demanded that she break off her old way.

As a sinner, her sin was squeezing the life out of her. She had felt powerless to stop the suffocating process. Now, because of Jesus, the Capernaum woman knew that she was no longer being stifled by self. Once a nonperson, she rejoiced that Jesus liberated her to be a person, freed her from whoredom to womanhood.

To her fellow townsfolk, however, she was still the town whore. She might have professed repentance because of Jesus the rabbi, but everyone except Jesus still looked on her with contempt.

When she crashed a dinner party given for Jesus by Simon the Pharisee, one of Capernaum's solid citizens, everyone gasped. Her one intention was to express her gratitude to Jesus. When she heard that Jesus was Simon's guest, she forgot her seedy reputation and ventured in. She meant to stay just a moment. What other time, she asked herself, would she have the opportunity to find Jesus and show her thanks.

She said nothing during the entire time she was in the room. Quietly, she slunk up behind Jesus. Jesus, reclining on his side—the way guests at a banquet always did—did not see her. Stretched out comfortably, sandals off and feet behind him, he was deep in conversation when the woman sneaked in.

The woman knelt down beside Jesus' feet. Taking the flask of *foliatum* (a perfume-like mixture of oil of roses and iris plants in a tiny jar commonly worn around the neck of every Jewish woman) she gently started to shake a few drops on his feet.

Suddenly and spontaneously, she started to cry. She could not control herself. Carried away with emotion, she could not stop her tears from dripping onto Jesus' feet. She was afraid that the tears would disturb him or, worse, defile him. Quickly, she wiped away the drops with a hank of her hair which had dropped.

As she dabbed at his feet, she bedewed them with more tears. Impulsively, the woman undid her hair and used the long tresses as a towel. She wept helplessly, burying her face in Jesus' feet and rubbing her hair over his ankles. Between sobs, she repeatedly kissed his feet.

Simon, the host, and all the guests except Jesus were appalled. No respectable woman ever unbraided her hair in public. Simon, a proper Pharisee, snorted at the disgusting scene. He waited, expecting Jesus to put an end to this shocking display of immodesty, and order the woman to leave.

When Jesus, saying nothing, patiently let the woman continue, Simon the Pharisee looked at Jesus with contempt. The curl on Simon's lip and frown on his forehead communicated his opinion of Jesus. "This man a prophet? Absurd! He should have recognized a prostitute when he saw one. No real prophet would allow such a despicable character to contaminate him. This Jesus obviously cannot read character, and a genuine prophet can!" Simon thought.

Jesus showed Simon the Pharisee that he certainly could read character. He read Simon's innermost thoughts—with embarrassing accuracy and clarity.

"A certain creditor had two debtors; one owed five hundred denarii," Jesus began.

Five hundred denarii! Everyone listened intently. Knowing that one denarius was the average daily wage, each guest realized what a fantastic sum, what a crushing debt Jesus was describing. Five hundred is a burden no working man could ever hope to pay off. His wages impounded and family deprived, the debtor Jesus spoke of would be hopelessly impoverished for life.

Jesus continued. "The other, fifty. . . ."

A debt of fifty denarii still put a man in desperate financial straits, everyone present nodded, although not as hopeless as the first fellow who owed five hundred.

Jesus wound up his story by telling that when they could not pay, the creditor made them each a gift, a free present, by cancelling their debts. "Which of them will love him more?" Jesus asked Simon (Luke 7:42).

Simon answered Jesus with a cavalier tone (the words, "I suppose," convey a superciliousness) implying Jesus was socially inferior. "The one, I suppose, to whom he forgave more" (7:43) Simon sniffed.

Worse, Simon had missed the point of the story about forgiveness and gratitude.

As a partial rebuke to Simon, the self-righteous Pharisee, Jesus turned to the woman while still speaking to Simon. Up until this time, Jesus had not looked at her.

"I was your invited guest," Jesus, in effect, said to Simon, "but you did not show any of the hospitality expected of a host, not even the simplest courtesies. This woman, on the other hand, did the honors due a guest."

The usual water for a foot bath? You, Simon, forgot it, but she did not. "She has wet my feet with her tears and wiped them with her hair" (7:44).

The kiss of greeting, the mark of respect and welcome due an eminent visiting rabbi? "You gave me no kiss, but from the time I came in, she has not ceased to kiss my feet" (7:45).

The customary soothing drops of aromatic oil on the guest's head before the meal begins? "You did not anoint my head with oil, but she has anointed my feet with ointment" (7:46).

"Therefore I tell you, her sins, which are many, are forgiven, for she loved much; but he who is forgiven little, loves little" Jesus coldly announced to Simon (7:47). (If you think you've sinned little, you will not sense much need of forgiveness. She knew how much she was forgiven, and therefore she loved.)

Simon, with his tidy Pharisee's "point system," imagined that his little goody-goody acts earned him God's favor. Actually, of course, like everyone else, he stood before God as a hopeless debtor.

We are not forgiven because we love. Rather, we love because we are forgiven.

Like life-giving rain to a fragile, wilting young stalk, Jesus' words to the ex-streetwalker reassured her that God accepted her. "Your sins are forgiven," he stated, using the verb form which means that her past has been forgiven and remains forgiven. He deliberately reinforced the woman's sense of being healed.

The woman brightened. Jesus had confirmed her assurance of being forgiven. Grateful beyond words (she said nothing during the entire interview) she realized that Jesus had publicly stated to everyone at the banquet—the elite of Capernaum—that she was a forgiven person. She knew that Jesus meant for her to return to society.

Rehabilitated by forgiveness mediated through Jesus, she no longer was a pseudoperson. Valued by God, she could then value herself.

Jesus looked at the seething host and guests. He could read their disgust. He heard them muttering, "Who is this, who even forgives sins?" (7:49).

Jesus chose an indirect approach to his critics by a direct approach to the woman. "Your faith has saved you," he tenderly reassured her. "Go in peace" (7:50).

Jesus' "Go in peace" is more than the usual *shalom* or Hebrew blessing. Literally, his words were, "Depart into peace!" He commended her to a lasting condition of peace, as a result of knowing God's acceptance of her, for as long as she lived in response to God's grace.

This "Go into peace" is promised to everyone who, responding to the divine Forgiver, trusts and obeys.

Do not, however, try to imagine that God's peace is a state of euphoria where you lay aside responsibilities. Some try to twist the gospel into being a hallucinogenic experience in which one is permitted to do as one pleases —even in matters of morals. In this age of increasing sexual permissiveness, there are also increasing pressures to declare marital fidelity obsolete. The woman of Capernaum, before her conversion, might today be voted Most Popular Girl for sharing her bed so willingly. When Actor Elliott Gould and pregnant Jenny Bogart walked out of the courtroom after his quickie divorce (from Barbra Streisand) announcing defiantly that they would continue to live together out of wedlock because "we don't believe in marriage," or when Northern Ireland's attractive, unmarried Bernadette Devlin went out of her way to let the press know that she expected a baby but added, "But my morals are a private matter," enticing voices were calling. The Capernaum bordello is still at hand. And Christ's peace will still be far away.

Under Christ's scrutiny, we all stand in need of forgiveness. Every man, like W. C. Fields sneering, "I believe in tying the marriage knot, as long as it's around the woman's neck," has exploited women in thought or deed. Every woman (at least secretly and at least some of the time) is hostile and resentful, like the woman of Capernaum, for being reduced to an object by a male-dominated culture. Both perish but for the undeserved, life-giving goodness of God.

Man and woman alike truly go into a state of peace (and, O God, how everyone needs Your peace!) when, grateful for God's grace, each shares God's kind of care and commitment to others!

THE TEEN-AGER
(Jairus's Daughter)

A pretty young thing, she had just passed "debutante age." Her coming-of-age party had been one of the social highlights of the year. Poised at the bright sunrise of adulthood, she was considered ready for marriage and grown-up responsibilities. She was twelve, the age when a Jewish girl passed legally into womanhood. (Jewish rules held that a girl should be regarded as a grown woman and accorded adult status at twelve years and one day, and marriage usually followed within a year or so in that culture.)

As an only child, the young lady was the pride and joy of her father, Jairus. She basked in the warmth of his personal affection. She also enjoyed the attention of being the daughter of a prominent, respected community leader who served as lay head of the leading local synagogue.

When she became ill, Jairus, her father, showed his usual concern. Her condition grew worse. The spectre of death seemed to creep into her bedroom. Her father became anxious.

At twelve, every day is important and beautiful for a girl. Emily Webb Gibbs in Thornton Wilder's *Our Town*, dead from complications of childbirth at a young age, is permitted to relive one day of her past and chooses her twelfth birthday. Ecstatically, she cries, "Oh earth, you're too wonderful for anyone to realize you! Do any human beings ever realize life while they live it?—every, every minute?"

The minutes on this wonderful earth were running out for Jairus's daughter. The black wind of the Pit seemed to swirl through her thinking. She lapsed into unconsciousness. Life was ebbing fast.

Hearing the girl giving her last gasps, the desperate father took drastic steps. Although as an official in the synagogue Jairus had criticized and opposed Jesus, he swallowed his pride and forgot his prejudices to go pleading to Jesus. He frantically shouldered his way through the crowd surrounding Jesus. Time was short. Without waiting for introductions, the distraught man quickly spilled out his story. "My little daughter," he gasped, "is at the point of death!" (Mark 5:23). His husky voice, tense mouth and strained eyes conveyed the extreme urgency he felt.

Jesus immediately sensed that Jairus was living a nightmare. Although he recognized Jairus as one of the hostile establishment, Jesus encouraged the man to continue speaking.

"Come," Jairus pleaded, "and lay your hands on her, so that she may be made well, and live." (5: 23).

Overcoming all his synagogue scruples about dealing with the heretic Jesus, Jairus appealed to Jesus as his last hope.

It was a delicious opportunity for Jesus to needle Jairus for coming crawling in his hour of need. How exquisitely pleasant it could have been to have made Jairus go through a long cross-examination about whether he took back the harsh words the synagogue leaders had said about Jesus' healings!

No grudges with Jesus, however. No sour grapes, no hurt feelings. Jesus graciously listened to the anxious father, Jairus.

No matter how inadequately or imperfect our reasons for coming to him, Jesus welcomes us. Our motives may be mixed, our faith wavering, and our theology confused. Nevertheless, he listens. Even though we might have scorned him or opposed him (and who hasn't?), he still accepts us. Just so we come!

Jesus immediately went with Jairus. Although Jesus had just returned from a long, exhausting trip and wanted rest, and although Jesus had a throng of eager listeners wanting him to continue his discourse, he accompanied Jairus. Jesus did not tell the desperate man to wait until it was convenient; nor irritated over this latest interruption, did Jesus snort and huff. Hopelessly inefficient by any modern industrial engineer's standards, Jesus constantly allowed himself to be distracted from systems and schedules. He dropped everything to meet Jairus's request. With Jesus, human need came ahead of inspiring sermons or his own comfort.

In this case, the human need was that of a girl. Nonetheless, Jesus insisted on accompanying Jairus.

Jesus' concern for the welfare of a young girl would have made bystanders' mouths drop open with surprise and scorn.

The Jewish community treated women as inferior. The rest of the first century world showed an appalling mercilessness toward women. A fragment of a letter dating to about A.D. 1 from a typical pagan businessman named Hilarion, to his wife, Alis, sums up the prevailing attitude. Away on a trip to Alexandria, Hilarion sends his greetings, then proceeds, "If—good luck be with you—you bear a child, if it is a boy, let it live; if it is a girl, throw it out."

Jesus, by contrast, cared about a young woman whom he had never met and whose father had treated him despicably!

As they walked toward Jairus's house, they were interrupted by an unfortunate woman with a longtime debilitating ailment. Jairus tensely clasped and unclasped his fingers, wanting to hurry Jesus on. His daughter's situation, he knew, was so desperate that they dare not delay a minute.

Suddenly someone from Jairus's house rushed up to tell him the crushing news. Jairus had been expecting it. When it came, however, he was devastated. Learning that his only child, his beloved girl, had been wrenched away from him by death, Jairus stood in the wound-shock of grief.

Even that doughty warrior of faith, Martin Luther, holding his dying fourteen-year-old daughter, Magdalena, in his arms, sobbed and found that in spite of all the blessings God had given, he could not find it in his heart to give thanks to God for anything. And after she was laid to rest, Luther, distraught with grief, cried, *"Du liebes Lenichen,* you will rise and shine like the stars and the sun. How strange it is to know that she is at peace and all is well, and yet be so sorrowful!"

Jairus's face was contorted with grief. He silently nodded his head as the messenger from home told him, "Your daughter is dead. Why trouble the Teacher any further?" (Mark 5:35).

Jesus overheard. Moving to Jairus's side, Jesus urged him not to give way to fear and worry. "Believe!" Jesus pleaded, and the verb form in the Greek means, *Keep on trusting me!* Even in the face of this new problem, God is not helpless!

"Dead" the expert testimony from the girl's bedside stated. Don't bother the Teacher any further. Case closed.

Not with God. No case ever is. God never tires of us or gives up on us. Man's "expert" testimony is never God's last word—even on the apparent extinction of the life of a young woman.

Nor is God ever at the end of his rope. Man—yes. But God—never!

Jesus kept on going. He would not be deterred by the report of the girl's death. When Jesus and Jairus reached Jairus's house, they discovered the report was true. Crowds of mourners and curiosity-seekers had collected already.

Inside the house, the frightening din of a typical Palestinian wake had begun. The usual hired mourners—women paid to shriek and wail and flail their arms—had set up their wild keening. The flute players were piping melancholic dirges.

(In Jewish, Greek, and Roman circles in the first century, death was so great and so final a calamity that normal outpourings of human emotion could not fully express grief. The Talmud, for example, insisted that at every funeral, "Even the poorest in Israel should hire not less than two flutes and one wailing woman.")

In addition to the exaggerated weeping and synthetic sorrow of the professional mourners, neighbors sobbed loudly. New arrivals quickly found themselves engulfed and overpowered by the emotion-packed scene. When Jesus and Jairus entered the house, they found the usual funeral customs being observed. All the careful protocol of death heightened the tragedy of the girl's untimely death.

Instead of following suit and joining in the sad clamor, as was expected, Jesus abruptly commanded everyone to hush and leave the house. Those in the house stood aghast, shocked at Jesus' lack of sympathy. How could Jesus be so unfeeling, so gauche?

Jesus, however, noted the way the flutes and shrieking women added to the family's misery. The funeral customs forced everyone to wallow in grief. Those present, Jesus observed, were made almost to feel resentful of any hope in God. Disgusted that sadness had been turned into a circus, he ordered everyone outside.

"Why do you make a tumult and weep?" Jesus demanded. His next words, however, brought howls of bitter, cynical laughter. "The child is not dead but sleeping" (Mark 5:39) Jesus stated.

Not dead but *sleeping!* This was too much for the half-hysterical crowd. Dammed-up emotions, cut off from the orgy of crying, suddenly exploded into uncontrolled paroxysms of laughing. To these present in Jairus's house, Jesus' words struck them as an absurd bit of gallows humor.

Paul Tillich sometimes commented that first century man was obsessed with Death; medieval man with guilt; and modern man with meaninglessness. Indeed, the first century people gathered that day in Jairus's home did have an obsession with Death. "And they laughed at him" (5:40). Everyone in that room knew all too well what Death was all about. What could Jesus do in the face of the final catastrophe—Death?

Death—the adversary which seized every strong man as well as a fragile girl on the threshold of womanhood—had won again. Death laughed obscenely with the people in Jairus's house. "I win every time," Death taunted; "Come on, take me on! The joke is on you, pretty young lady! No matter who you are—daughter of the synagogue head man or town leader —I, Death, touch everything with absurdity!"

God, however, has the last laugh! He even turns the tables on Death. God with a conclusive chuckle overrules the worst of human circumstances!

Entering the death chamber with the girl's parents and his three trusted friends, Peter, James and John, Jesus instilled new life in the young woman!

No *abracadabra*. No dramatic flourishes. No spooky touches. Nor any flashy details. Gently, as if waking her from a deep sleep, Jesus told the girl to get up. The three Synoptic Gospel accounts record the episode (the only case of raising from the dead reported by all three), but Mark reported the exact Aramaic words. *Talitha cumi* (5:41) Jesus said, perhaps using the tender terms of endearment used in most Palestinian homes. Possibly *Talitha cumi* was the caressing phrase which Jesus heard Mary say to waken her family each morning. "C'mon, my little lambie, it's time to get up," Jesus quietly urged.

Jesus' strength and serenity stand in juxtaposition to the mourners' puniness and panic. The One who effected the death of Death conferred new life for Jairus's daughter for everyone present that day. Jesus has power to awaken! This is why he spoke of death as a "sleep."

Startlingly, Jesus even touched the girl's corpse. "Taking her by the hand," (5:41) meant polluting himself. Nothing was more defiling, nothing more dangerous than handling the dead. The book of Leviticus spells out the strict rules and dread warnings. Jesus took the risks; Jesus broke the rules.

Jesus literally made contact with the final adversary. In the room of a young woman of Capernaum, Jesus came to grips with Death. And Jesus demonstrated his command even over that conqueror!

Significantly, Jesus immediately showed a down-to-earth practicality and concern. Instead of striking a pious pose (with eyes upturned) and uttering platitudes about "spiritual" matters, Jesus turned to the girl's parents and told them to get her something to eat!

No other-wordliness with Jesus! Unlike some of his modern followers who insist on discussing "souls," Jesus cares about bodies, too. "Give her something to eat," he instructed (5:43). He had a concern about the girl's physical health, about her nourishment and concern about her biological processes.

Don't try to rationalize this episode, as some commentators do. Occasionally, someone will minimize the event by saying that the girl was not dead but sleeping. It is useless to try to "prove" that the young woman suffered a seizure, or slipped into a coma or a cataleptic trance, because the medical details are too skimpy. Furthermore, the bystanders did not suppose that the girl had died; they *knew* that she was dead (see Luke 8:53). And dead or not, Jesus rescued her from her funeral and entombment. Burial always took place on the day of death, and occasional archaeological evidence in tombs shows that it was not uncommon for people to be buried alive while unconscious, only to revive later. Even if it were true that Jairus's daughter had not actually died, Jesus saved her from the ghastly experience of being laid away in the Pit.

> Make haste to answer me, O Lord!
> My spirit fails!
> Hide not thy face from me,
> lest I be like those who go down
> to the Pit.
> Psalm 143:7

So goes an ancient Jewish prayer which Jairus's daughter often heard.

In Jesus Christ, God personally answered her. In the person of the Teacher of Nazareth, God turned his face toward Jairus's daughter. He pulled her back from the Pit. Later, in fact, he literally went through the Pit-experience himself for her—and for all girls. Our God who has reached down into the Pit and resurrected Jesus Christ insistently bestows new life on our daughters.

There are various forms of the Pit. And there are various ways of sleeping away one's existence and slipping away from life. No Pit is too deep for God. The enlivening Presence of God through Jesus brought back Jairus's daughter from one form of the Pit. And He acts to liberate from any Pit any girl who gives up on herself, on reality, on the world or who even gives up on Him!

As parents, we must invite Him to come home with us to communicate life to our daughters. If our girls do not encounter in our homes the love which was embodied in Jesus Christ, they are almost inevitably sentenced to some kind of Pit, whether it be promiscuity, drugs, running away, psychosis, or boredom with living.

In *A Tale of Two Cities*, the deathcarts trundle their daily loads of victims to the guillotine during the bloody madness of the French Revolution. A young, orphaned seamstress marked for execution sits beside Sydney Carton, the nonhero hero of Dickens's novel, as the tumbrel bumps its way through the jeering Paris street mobs. Noticing the girl's fright and loneliness, Carton gently takes her trembling hand and comforts her. Strengthened by Carton's compassionate presence through the horrible final journey, the girl looks up at Carton and smiles, "I think you were sent to me by Heaven."

Apply these words to Jesus Christ the Messiah.

What better expression of the meaning of His coming! With His power and His presence, every person—woman or man—is delivered from every form of the Pit!

THE UNWANTED
(Woman With a Hemorrhage)

Her invalid's face with its worry lines and sickroom pallor made her look much older than she was. Her eyes, rinsed with years of pain, blinked pleadingly. Her thin body sagged with weariness. When she moved, she walked slowly, as a person in great discomfort. Twelve years of constant illness and doctoring had turned her into a prematurely-aged crone.

Her ailment was not only debilitating but embarrassingly personal. For twelve years, the unfortunate woman had suffered from uterine bleeding. Her constant hemorrhaging could have been caused by fibroid tumors, or an endocrine gland disturbance causing irregular bleeding such as hypertrophic endometritis (overgrowth of the endometrium) due to dysfunctioning of the ovaries, or an inflammation or an abscess or tear in the cervix, or it could have been a polyp. She lived with constant pain and dread.

Worse, she had to endure the humiliation of being considered ceremonially unclean.

To the ancients, there was a deep sense of disgust and embarrassment over bodily excretions, particularly from the area associated with sexual functions. Any kind of uterine discharge, including menstrual flow, automatically rendered a woman unclean.

Cleanness was connected with holiness. Israel, according to Jewish tradition, had to reject any uncleanness, or God would turn away His face. The nation's survival, it was taught, depended on purity in every form. Consequently, Jewish Law had strict and detailed regulations about clean and unclean. Many of these regulations, of course, are known today to be sound hygienic procedures.

Leviticus 15:19–27 specified that everything an unclean woman touched —including her bed, her clothing and all utensils—was considered polluted. Furthermore, any other person coming in contact with an unclean woman was also contaminated, and was required to go through elaborate purifying ceremonies. After a woman completed her menstrual period, she could not be considered clean again until a prescribed cleansing bath.

For twelve years, this particular woman had suffered the indignity of being considered unclean. She could not take part in any of the Jewish feasts or holy days. Marriage, of course, was an impossibility. Ostracized by others because of her unclean condition, she developed many of the symptoms of psychosis which a person acquires when cut off from normal contact with society. The woman, separated from others and from public religious practices, suspected that she was also shunned by God.

Desperately, she tried to get relief from her disorder. She quickly exhausted the folk remedies suggested by other women in her village. She sought out medical help.

First-century medical lore could do little for a woman with uterine bleeding. The treatments were frequently gruesome and revolting. Pliny's *Natural History* reports that the prescription for such a problem consisted of applying a poultice of fresh donkey manure and making the patient drink goat urine. Other remedies were simply quackery, such as carrying the ashes from a charred ostrich egg in a little linen sack in summer, and in a cotton rag in winter. Another "cure" for vaginal hemorrhage consisted of carrying at all times a grain of barley retrieved from the droppings of a white she-ass.

Even the Jewish medical knowledge failed to help her. She submitted to such therapeutics as the following described on one leaf of the *Talmud*.

Rabbi Jochanan said, "Bring [or take] gum of Alexandria the weight of a zuzee, and of alum, the weight of a zuzee, and of crocus hortensis the weight of a zuzee. Let these be crushed together and given in wine to the woman who has an issue of blood . . . But if this does not benefit, take of Persian onions three logs, boil them in wine, then give her to drink, and say, 'Arise from your flux.' But if this does not prevail, set her in a place where two roads meet, and let her hold a cup of wine in her hand, and let someone come up behind her and frighten her and say, 'Arise from your flux?' But if it does no good, take a handful of cumin and a handful of crocus and a handful of foenum graecum. Let these be boiled in wine, and give them to her to drink, and say, 'Arise from your flux.' But if these do not benefit, and other doses are still prescribed, in number ten or more, which see, if you please, in the place cited. Among them, I cannot omit this: Let them dig seven ditches, in which let them burn cuttings of such vines as are not circumcised (not yet four years old). And let her take in her hand a cup of wine. And let them lead her away from the ditch, and make her sit down over that. And let them remove her from that, and make her sit down over another. And in every removal you must say to her, 'Arise from your flux.' "

Of the eleven remedies proposed by this learned rabbi, six are astringents administered as tonics. The rest are merely superstition.

After twelve years of such sickening doses and torturous treatments, the woman found herself no better. In fact, her condition had grown worse, the pain and discomfort were more severe, aggravated by years of "remedies." Deeply depressed, the woman had made the rounds of all of the medical resources she could find. Reluctantly, she concluded that no doctor could help her.

At the end of twelve years, she not only found herself more miserable than before, but broke as well. Both her health and the means of regaining her health were gone. She had used up all her resources, spent her savings, pawned her valuables and exhausted her credit in her quest for medical help.

Pale, shrunken, and weak, the woman with the hemorrhage resigned herself to living without hope and without money to provide hope.

Even the gospel writer Luke, himself a physician, acknowledged that this was a hopeless case, medically speaking, and reported frankly that she "could not be healed by anyone" (Luke 8:43).

Eusebius, a learned bishop in the early church, referring to Caesarea-Philippi, mentions that this is the hometown of the unfortunate woman with the hemorrhage (*Ecclesiastical History*, VII:18). If this is the case, the woman traveled nearly thirty miles—a considerable journey on foot for an invalid—to Capernaum to meet Jesus.

She had heard reports of his wondrous cures. Mindful of her own condition, she resolved to meet him. She convinced herself that Jesus could relieve some of her distress. With a determination born of desperation, she painfully made her way to Capernaum.

To her dismay, however, she discovered that Jesus was thronged every waking hour. Her plans to find him alone for a personal interview to avoid embarrassment had to be abandoned. In fact, she quickly saw that Jesus had no privacy himself. Everyone in Galilee, it seemed to her, had brought an ailing relative or friend to him for healing.

The jostling and noise, the heat and the long hours on her feet made her feel faint. As the days passed and she still had not been able to get near Jesus to speak to him, the tiny sum of money she had managed to scrape together for the trip began to run out. Soon, she would have no funds—and still no health.

If only she could just get near enough to Jesus to speak to him for a minute, she told herself. But it would have to be soon. She barely had enough coins to buy her bread and lodging for another couple of days. And every morning seemed to bring greater crowds into Capernaum. The woman with the hemorrhage realized that she was competing against larger numbers each day. Every person, she noted with dismay, seemed to have some favor to ask of Jesus.

Meanwhile, she tried to avoid coming in contact with others, knowing that her condition made her unclean. Ashamed to divulge her ailment to others, she cringed on the edge of the crowds swirling around Jesus. She felt like a nonperson.

She told herself, "If only I could get near enough to Jesus to touch even one of the tassels on his garment, I am certain I'd be healed!" Although she knew that this would make Jesus unclean, she rationalized that it wouldn't be as bad because he would never even know anyone had touched him. She plotted how she would creep up surreptitiously when he was not looking. Just let a tassel brush her hand, she assured herself, and she would be cured.

Although she was prohibited from mingling in the crowd because the Law decreed that she contaminated everyone she came into contact with, she risked breaking the Law. This was her last opportunity for healing. Jesus was her final effort to get relief.

Trying to get to Jesus that day was like trying to swim up a roaring cataract, but the woman persisted. She grimly fought off waves of dizziness. Tortured by fatigue and guilt, she considered abandoning her plan and accepting defeat.

Suddenly, she saw the Master coming through the crowds in her direction. The hemorrhaging woman furtively made her way among the people pressing around Jesus until she was directly behind him.

She stealthily extended her hand and gingerly touched a *zizith*, one of the four tassels on the corners of a Jewish male's outergarment. She was certain that she had not attracted any notice, because she had touched a *zizith* hanging over Jesus' shoulder, and he had not seen her. It was the least possible contact.

But her private scheme for a cure worked! Instantly, she felt in her body that all was well. The hemorrhage had stopped! (Luke, in 8:44, employed the correct medical term as usual. "Immediately," he reported, "her flow of blood ceased," using the surgeon's word to describe the cessation of bodily discharge.)

Did Jesus feel the imperceptible jerk on one of his *ziziths?* Did he half-consciously sense the nervous presence of the unfortunate woman? Or, had he caught a glimpse of her out of the corner of his eye as she slunk up?

In any case, he felt suddenly drained of energy. He seemed to know intuitively that he had empowered someone, showing that his healings always cost because they always drained him of strength. Jesus constantly gave of himself.

Immediately stopping and turning around, Jesus asked, "Who touched my garments?" (Mark 5:30).

His disciples tried to point out that there were so many people crowding around him that it was impossible to find who had touched him.

Furthermore, his disciples were trying to hurry Jesus along to answer an emergency call. A little girl, the daughter of Jairus the head man of the local synagogue, lay dying, and it was urgent that Jesus get to the house as soon as possible. The disciples, especially Peter, were annoyed that Jesus was trying to single out the one who had touched him. Tapping their fingers anxiously they wanted to rush on to the bedside of Jairus's little girl.

Most of us resent interruptions. We regard anyone who intrudes on our schedule or distracts us from our plans as a nuisance.

Not Jesus. He was never "too busy." He never found himself unable to cope. He was always able to reorganize his time. For him, interruptions were opportunities.

Jesus, disregarding the nervous glances of his disciples and the noisy confusion of the crowd, looked and looked and kept looking for the person who had touched him. Obviously, he sensed that someone had touched him deliberately and meaningfully. He seemed to know that someone was communicating nonverbally.

The woman saw that Jesus was looking for her. She desperately wanted to hide. She could not bear to be exposed in public as an unclean woman. The whole world would know that she had broken the Law. She could not face the humiliation of exposing her shame. Trying to melt into the masses pushing and jostling around her, she thought at first that she had succeeded in evading detection.

The woman discovered, however, that she was not hidden. A moment before, she had imagined that she had found the perfect hiding place from Jesus—being part of an enormous, faceless horde of humanity. Even the camouflage of a crowd, she learned, could not conceal her from the searching Saviour.

No person hides from God. "If I take the wings of the morning and dwell in the uttermost parts of the sea . . ." (or zoom to the farther side of the moon . . . or consider myself a nameless cypher among the anonymous millions of faces around me), ". . . thou hast searched me and known me . . . thou discernest my thoughts from afar" (Psalm 139).

Happily found, the woman shyly stepped forward. For a few moments, she felt that she was the only one present with Jesus. In spite of the people crowding around, she believed that she was the only one who mattered.

Although his time was precious and although he was faced with an emergency, Jesus gave this woman his total and undivided attention. He ignored the pressures by his disciples and the clock and the masses for the one unfortunate, unclean outcast. His actions embodied his message, "It is not the will of my Father who is in heaven that one of these little ones should perish" (Matthew 18:14).

As Augustine said years later, "God loves each of us as if there were only one of us to love!"

Significantly, the woman's religion was a blend of superstition, trust, and cunning. It was not a mature faith. In fact, it bordered on magic. Her scheme to appropriate healing by touching a tassel of Jesus' garb reveals a childish effort to manipulate the divine for her own ends.

Tentative and immature though the woman's faith was, Jesus willingly received her. She did not have to flash theological credentials before he noticed her. He accepted the woman where she was. He gave her the confidence to be honest with him. And when she spilled out the pathetic details of her case history over the past twelve years, he listened attentively.

When he spoke to her, Jesus chose one of the tenderest words in any language. "Daughter," he called her. Although she was probably not much younger and perhaps even older than Jesus, Jesus instead of speaking to her as a man to a woman, gently and thoughtfully addressed her like a father to a little girl.

"Take heart (meaning literally, "Courage" or "Have confidence" and meaning roughly the same as "Keep the faith, baby!"), my daughter; your faith has made you well" (Matthew 9:22). See also Mark 5:34, Luke 8:48.

Jesus ignored her superstition and cunning. He accented the positive, built on the good aspects of her actions, and developed her attempt to trust him. "Your faith has made you well," or, as the Greek verb tense literally means, "Your faith has just saved you and the effects of your faith continue even now!" Jesus assured her that she was permanently cured.

Bidding her farewell, Jesus told her, "Go into peace." The *shalom* passed as a Jewish greeting, however, means more to Jesus than simply "peace." The *shalom* of God stands for health and general well-being.

Traditions are unanimous that the woman went into peace and lived in

God's *shalom*. Veronica (the name of the woman, according to one ancient report) returned to Caesarea-Philippi (her home, according to legends passed on by Eusebius). There, as one old story has it, Veronica erected a bronze statue of a woman on bended knee, her hands outstretched imploringly. Opposite this sculpture, stood another figure, of the Saviour, whose arms extended compassionately toward the woman. Before the statues grew a plant, carefully tended by Veronica, which was a marvelous antidote to many diseases.

Legend or truth? Who knows? Whatever the facts about the subsequent career of the woman with the hemorrhage who was liberated from her humiliating, debilitating ailment by Jesus, she went home with *shalom!*

THE WEEPER
(Widow of Nain)

John Donne penned a funeral elegy in which he wrote that Death is the sea which surrounds us. Although God has put bounds on it, we always hear its roar and feel it gnawing at our shores.

For a certain woman in an obscure Palestinian village called Nain, death's waves seemed always to be eroding the coastline of her existence.

First, her husband had been carried away. She had wept for days, cried until her tearducts dried, until the heaving sobs no longer racked her and she could only moan.

At first, her friends had rallied. A few days after the funeral, however, they drifted back to their own families and seemed to expect her to assume that life would revert to its normal routine for everyone.

Life, she knew, would never revert to normal for her. She often found herself half-expecting her man to walk in at his usual time just before dinner, and sighed as she remembered again that he never would. Sometimes, she startled herself by noticing how a stranger resembled her husband or some man had a mannerism which reminded her of her spouse. She would reminisce and brood for hours.

For a long time, the widow had tortured herself by blaming herself at least in part for her husband's death. Suppose she had done this, or what if she had said that? And she would lament her failures. Occasionally, she would feel particularly blue when she remembered the times when she had not been as responsive or patient as she might have been with him.

Every part of daily living reminded her of the life she had once shared. When she set the table, she had to remember not to set his place. When she stretched out to go to sleep, she heard no whispered *Good-night.* Each holiday, she discovered afresh how lonely it could be without her man to plan with or celebrate with.

Fortunately, she had a son, their only child. This living link with her husband became the focus of her existence.

She scratched out a meagre subsistence for the youngster and herself, pouring all her energies into the boy's welfare. Although often exhausted from the burden of providing for the lad, she comforted herself with the thought that eventually he would be able to look after them both. She willingly went without dinners so that he would have enough to eat. In a few years, she knew, he would step into the adult male role of breadwinner. She endured the grim privations of being a widow, assuring herself that they would only be temporary.

When the boy entered young manhood and began to earn a living for them both, she felt the economic pressures finally start to ease. She began to enjoy reasonably comfortable declining years, with the security of an able-bodied son bringing home the groceries each evening. She even allowed herself to dream of her son marrying, of grandchildren, of the joys of the sunset years by being surrounded with family.

Suddenly, like a mighty wave washing unexpectedly high on the beach, Death, the surrounding sea, carried away her son.

Once again, the woman carried out the conventionalities of mourning. She let her hair fall disheveled. She ripped her undergarment, reversed it, then tore her dress in front. She let her face go unwashed. She sat on the floor. She refused meat and wine. Abandoning herself to grief, she did not even offer the usual prayer before eating. She sobbed and moaned, trying to express her grief.

In Palestinian culture, there was no more terrible sorrow than a childless widow. The entire community reinforced her sense of tragedy. The name of the village, Nain, meant "the pleasant place," but every resident knew that for the widow who had just lost her only son, the place would never again be pleasant. Without her son as a means of support, the woman was doomed to be destitute as well as desolate. Everyone understood the ramifications of the young man's death.

The news carried. The blast of the horn told nearby villages that a tragedy had struck. People dropped what they were doing and hurried to Nain.

Some of the neighbor ladies performed the brief undertaking chores. They washed the young man's body, trimmed his nails and hair, and tied shut his jaw and eyelids before rigor mortis set in. Gently, they asked the woman for the tiny but expensive jar of ointment which she had been hoarding for her own burial, and rubbed the aromatic oil on the corpse of her son. Finally, they wrapped the body in the best sheet the widow owned, leaving only the face exposed.

Looking at her son's dead body, the mother's face contorted and she sobbed uncontrollably. She saw the lifeless waxen face and remembered the excitement and hopes she had felt years before when she first discovered she was going to have her baby. She recalled the discomforts and jokes with her husband while she was carrying her son—the day when her labor pains began—it seemed so recent and yet so long ago. She recalled her anxiety —the rough solicitude and efficient care of the older neighbor wives, some of whom were helping now to lay out the body of the boy they helped bring into the world. She remembered the feel of the tiny, squalling, warm living thing in her arms just after he was born—her tiredness and contentment at that moment—the wonder and exhilaration that only a mother having a baby can appreciate—the awe and gratitude to the Creator and Bestower of life.

In her grief, the woman of Nain thought of the times she had sat up all night when the boy had been ill—the morning he started to crawl—his first steps—the day he surprised her by saying, "Mamma!" She thought of his favorite toys. How he had grown! Suddenly he had been as tall as she, she recalled. She remembered her surprise when she noticed the size of his hands one day—when his voice changed—when his beard started to sprout. But now, he lay *dead.* Stricken and alone, the widow buried her head in her hands and wept and wept.

The hired mourners arrived (it was customary to pay at least one woman to wail and two flute players to screech morosely) and set up their incessant sounds of sorrow. The young man's death was so sad, however, no one needed the stimulus to grieve provided by the professional mourners.

A couple of neighbors made arrangements to have a grave prepared because burial had to take place before sundown. Others brought the wicker-frame device used to carry the dead. Only the rich could afford a carved cedarwood open coffin. The peasants in Nain, like most Palestinians, bore their dead to the cemetery in a simple wicker receptacle.

Finally, the preparations for the burial of the widow's son were completed. Everyone in Nain and the surrounding area gathered. Not to join the funeral procession was to show disrespect toward the deceased and to mock God. No one in Nain dared show such irreverence. Custom decreed that all work—even study—had to be dropped when someone in the village died.

The hired mourners wailed louder. One woman would start singing a phrase, chanting such words as, "Alas the hero! Alas the lion!" and the others would join in, improvising a chorus in a sad minor key. The flutes shrilled their loud, quavering lamentations, accompanying the singers by ascending and descending the scale in quarter tones and halftones. The man selected as the funeral orator began to recite all the complimentary remarks about the widow's son he could think of, preparatory to his long eulogy at the grave. The corpse was lifted on to the wicker bier. The first shift of pallbearers took hold of the frame and lifted it to their shoulders. The procession started to move toward the village cemetery, called "the field of weepers" in all Palestinian towns.

First came the professional wailers and flute players, pouring out their dolorous music in shrieking crescendos. Next came the orator, intoning the outstanding deeds and character traits of the dead son of the widow. Just in front of the wicker bier, pathetically alone, walked the widow. Behind her, a group of men carried the dead son in the wicker frame. As a sign of mourning, these men had removed their sandals and walked barefoot. All the able-bodied men in the village were anxious to show their respect to the deceased by serving as pallbearers, so they took turns carrying the bier. Each time a new group took over bearing the wickerwork device, the entire multitude exhibited its grief with a fresh outpouring of sobs and shrieks. Saddened villagers from Nain and sympathizers from the outlying area trailed behind the pallbearers.

Jesus and a group of his followers happened to meet the funeral procession. Jewish etiquette was quite clear; it was Jesus' duty as a pious Jew to join the procession of mourners and show his respect for the dead man by accompanying the body to its tomb.

Jesus, always perceptive, observed all the details of the scene. What particularly caught his eye was the widow from Nain. Jesus saw instantly that the stricken woman was alone and elderly—and desperate. He knew that with her only son dead she would be deprived of her only means of livelihood. There were no pensions, no social security checks, no old people's homes. Destitute widows eked out bare survival by relying on handouts and pawning their meagre possessions, and eventually succumbed to exhaustion and malnutrition.

Jesus' reaction? Merely perform the perfunctory by joining the procession? Not Jesus. "When the Lord saw her, he had compassion on her" (Luke 7:13). The word in Greek for "he had compassion" is freighted with extra meaning. Coming from the root word for the organs in the lower abdomen, the idea in Greek is that Jesus had deep visceral feelings of pity, was moved to the very depths of his being. The modern slang saying, "He felt sorry for her on a gut-level," expresses the Greek most literally!

Jesus was moved with compassion for a person whom he had never seen before—an insignificant, near-penniless widow from an obscure back-country village miles from his own home!

Compare this with other faiths and cults. Stoicism, the most popular philosophy of the first century, and the Eastern religions sneered at compassion. According to these religions, the universe and all heavenly powers remained apathetic to lonely, grieving widows in Palestinian villages. The deities stood aloof and detached, unmoved and unconcerned. The best that the Stoics and the Eastern holy men could advocate was "Life is tough, but so what? Try to accept your lot as well as you can."

In the life of Jesus, God disclosed his character traits. Through Jesus' acts, we understand God's personality. And we know that God feels for us on a "gut-level." God had compassion for all hurting people. In the episode of Jesus encountering a widow sobbing in her son's funeral procession, we learn the depths of God's concern for us and all lonely, frightened persons.

Furthermore, his compassion is more than emotion or sentiment. Jesus got involved. His compassion was always expressed in specific ways. He insisted on converting his emotions into action. Moreover, Jesus translated his feelings by going out of his way for women, for the poor, for the weak, for the forgotten.

The common formula at funerals in Palestine was "Weep with them all ye who are bitter of heart." Instead of participating in the outburst of emotion, Jesus commanded the widow, "Do not weep!" (Luke 7:13). Jesus was sure of himself and certain of what was going to happen by speaking so strongly and positively.

Next, Jesus put out his hands, touching the bier and the shrouded corpse, to make the procession stop. When Jesus handled the dreaded object, he knowingly broke a terrifying taboo. The Jewish rule stated, "He who touches the dead body of any person shall be unclean seven days" (Numbers 19:11), and laid down complicated procedures to be followed before the person violating the law may be permitted to take part in Jewish worship again. Jesus willingly put himself out and interfered with the march to the grave.

Some contemporary Bible commentaries suggest that Jesus diagnosed the situation as a case of a young man being in a deep cataleptic seizure or lying in a coma. It is impossible to debate the subject since there were no electroencephalograms taken, no death certificates written. Those present that day in the village of Nain insisted that the young man had died. In any event, they were on their way to bury him. Even if he had not actually died, Jesus kept him from being interred alive. Everyone agrees that Jesus claimed for life a man marked for death.

Addressing the young man, Jesus ordered authoritatively, "Young man, I say to you, arise" (Luke 7:14). The Greek word "to you" is an emphatic form of address and underlines Jesus' insistent command. It is as if Jesus shouted, *"You!* You wrapped in that shroud, get up!"

The widow's son sat up (and Luke used the medical word for a patient sitting up in bed) and started to speak (confirming that he was indeed alive and in full control of all of his faculties).

Jesus did not try to make himself out as a super-Houdini, a better-than-average trickster. Unlike the fakirs, showmen, quacks and miracle mongers roaming the first century world, Jesus performed no stunts. Others also claimed to "raise the dead" and used their raisings as props to boost their cults. Some flashy personalities such as Apollonius emphasized the weird and accented the sensational to build huge followings. In each case, their raisings took place after mysterious incantations, extravagant gestures, and secret spells. Not with Jesus. Jesus refused to cater to the crowds shouting for a trick. He avoided the trappings of magic. No exploiting the supernatural; no performing for the masses.

Nor did Jesus try to prove his power. He consistently refused to use miracles to prove his uniqueness or to clinch his followers' faith. The miracles do not explain Jesus. Rather, Jesus explains the miracles.

The miracle is God's love—is Jesus himself! What should astonish us about what happened during a funeral procession at Nain is not the resuscitation of a man in a shroud. Rather, what *should* grab us is Jesus' involvement! The clinical details of the man being revived are relatively minor. (In fact, to the first-century Jews, raising the dead was no more impossible than healing a leper.) Jesus' wondrous act of compassion, Jesus' incredible demonstration of concern—this is the miracle!

All the recorded instances of Jesus raising the dead were done for the sake of women (Jairus's daughter, Mary and Martha's brother, and the widow of Nain's son). The miraculous aspect is Jesus' care for women. Instead of turning aside apathetically from women—as every guru and sect of the time advocated—Jesus actively and insistently allied himself with women's hurts and needs and loneliness. For the sake of women, the Prince of Life encountered the Power of Death. The Liberator met the Captor.

In the case of the widow of Nain, Jesus knew her needs—food, shelter, companionship. He cared so much about her that he interrupted the graveyard march to give her back her son. Raising her son from the bier was love acted out. The focus is on Jesus and his kind of caring. The real miracle is Jesus' concern for the well-being of a helpless lady whose only means of support was gone.

After Jesus raised the man from the bier, he further astonished those in the funeral procession by instructing the man to return to Nain and continue to look after his mother. Anyone but Jesus would have claimed the man as Exhibit A. After all, what better proof of Jesus' prowess than flesh-and-blood evidence of the man snatched from the grave? Jesus, however, refused to exploit the widow's son. Instead of taking the young man with him to dazzle the crowds, Jesus "gave him to his mother" (Luke 7:15). Jesus, compassionate as always, insisted that the widow have the young man's support.

Jesus bestowed new life for both the widow and the son. He not only reanimated the young man's lifeless body but revitalized the mother's empty existence.

No wonder everyone present that day shouted, "God has visited his people!" (Luke 7:16), using the special word for a physician visiting a patient. In Jesus Christ, God visited an anonymous widow from an obscure hick town named Nain. The nameless widow and little Nain stand for every woman, every town.

Little known and hardly remembered though you may think yourself, God has visited His people. And you are one of His people.

Through Jesus Christ, God has stepped directly into human existence, touching your life with joy and hope. The gospel is the news that your career on earth is not a dreary procession of yesterdays ending with a moderate-price funeral. Just when you may write *The End*, God inserts His own *To Be Continued* and turns the page!

Christ liberates you from the deadly grip of grief.

Therefore, although you may know on a visceral level the truth of Masefield's lines:

> *Life is bitter to the very bone*
> *When is woman, poor and alone . . .*

you need not withdraw into yourself, so that your existence becomes all mirrors and no windows. Because of the news that Jesus radically affected the funeral procession of the widow of Nain's son, and because of the news that God interrupted Jesus' nonexistence with the Resurrection, you may stop your whimpering. You may wipe your eyes. You may even help spread the exhilarating announcement that God continues to visit His people!

THE TIRED HOUSEWIFE

(Woman Unable to Stand Straight)

For eighteen years she had been so stooped that she resembled a grotesque gnome. She hobbled awkwardly rather than walked, and used a heavy stick to keep herself from falling forward on her face. Shoulders hunched and neck bent downward, she faced the ground like a grazing animal.

Every simple chore turned into a painful and laborious project. Filling a water jug at the village well, carrying it to her cottage, gathering fuel for her fire, bringing grain from the market, grinding her flour, baking her bread and tending her garden—all the womanly tasks took immense effort and left her panting and aching.

Even sleep came hard. Unable to straighten her misshapen body, she lay on one side until she woke, cramped and stiff, then with great effort turned herself to her other side for another snatch of rest.

The woman's condition had continued for eighteen years—the best part of her productive years. She often felt useless. She wondered what it would be like to be free from pain, to feel wanted. After eighteen years, life had declined into the predictable routine known as Getting Through the Day.

"She was bent over and could not fully straighten herself," physician-author Luke reports (13:11). In other words, she was not really standing up, nor at the same time was she helplessly lying down. She could not move about freely, yet she was not totally immobilized.

Twisted like a human pretzel so that her eyes were on the ground, she learned after eighteen years not to look up in any way. Her horizons were literally and figuratively the bumps on the path a few steps ahead. Her gaze was locked on her feet. Her view of life and the universe was completely earthbound. Anyone who never sees the stars and always looks at the dust quickly loses perspective, and the woman bent double acquired a distorted outlook on everything, including herself. She did not so much ask why she was dying as wonder why she was living.

Although she had sought medical attention, she had not been helped. Luke the doctor in his terse case-history gospel prose diagnosed her condition as a "spirit of infirmity" (13:11). In other words, her condition had no physical origin, but was psychosomatically caused. Crippled by a malign power, the woman found herself tethered physically as well as emotionally.

Jesus had the extraordinary capacity of moving on all these levels to free people from a "spirit of infirmity."

He noticed the bent-over woman, although she did not notice him.

Limping clumsily, head poked downward at an absurd angle, the woman saw nothing but the worn entrance to the little village synagogue and the feet of a few nearby worshipers. She intended to make her way as unobtrusively as possible to the women's section.

Sustained by the Promise, the ancient pact with the God who committed Himself to His people, the woman hoped to participate again in her people's act of listening-obeying. It was the Sabbath, the period between sundown Friday to sundown Saturday, when pious Jews celebrated the blessed break from toil given their ancestors who had been worked to death in the Egyptian brickyards. True, Sabbath had come to be freighted with burdensome rules, but the woman with the hairpin-spine looked forward to the worship and rest it brought. She never suspected that this Sabbath would also bring relief from eighteen years of misery.

She was surprised to hear someone addressing her. After eighteen years of being ignored or at best tolerated as a deformed freak, the woman did not expect anyone to speak to her with genuine warmth and interest. Her world of feet and paths had not included faces with smiles and conversation.

"Woman," the friendly voice speaking to her continued, "you are freed from your infirmity" (Luke 13:12).

"Freed!" This is the only place in the New Testament where this Greek word is used in regard to illness. Here, having special medical meaning, it is the technical term to describe the process in which taut tendons are relaxed.

Luke, precise as always, commented that Jesus empowered the woman to relax the contracted muscles of her chest which kept her hunched forward. Medically, however, releasing the tensed tendons and tissue would not enable the woman to stand with erect posture.

Throwing all the rules of propriety to the winds, Jesus stepped over and gently took hold of the woman with his hands. He disregarded the shocked looks and murmurs of disapproval. He knew well that he was smashing longstanding traditions by (a) daring to touch a woman (something no self-respecting Jew, particularly a rabbi, would ever be seen doing); (b) breaking the Sabbath by "working."

The woman felt strong, sure carpenter's hands firmly gripping her. "Immediately, she was made straight," Luke reported (13:13), employing the medical expression for removing a curvature or straightening a dislocated part of the body to its natural position.

The woman stretched. Delightedly, she found that she had been strengthened to stand tall and straight. No longer bent and twisted like an aged, gnarled tree on a windswept cliff, the woman assumed human appearance. She felt alive, she felt human for the first time in eighteen years.

Spontaneously, she broke into an improvised doxology. She had to express her sense of freedom and joy! Her impromptu praises glorifying God filled the tiny synagogue.

Nearly everybody, including Jesus, smiled appreciatively. One important looking man did not smile. Scowling, this man—the ruler or elected official of the synagogue—strutted pompously to the center. Irate because Jesus had healed the woman on the Sabbath, the ruler waited for the hubbub of excitement to subside. He did not protest to Jesus, however; instead he whined self-righteously to the worshipers that the rules about the Sabbath had been broken. "There are six days on which work ought to be done; come on those days and be healed, and not on the sabbath day."

The synagogue ruler's words stung the woman like a lash. She could not help but take them personally. Although the leader's speech had been directed at everyone present, she sensed that he had been speaking primarily to her. She cringed, and turned.

The woman, so buoyant and elated a few moments earlier, felt punctured. Involuntarily, her shoulders began to droop.

Of course, she remembered, it was the Sabbath, and the tight rules about not working on the Sabbath had been broken. She was guilty and so was the rabbi who had healed her.

Jesus exploded with words that sear and scorch. Never for a moment imagine that Jesus is a perpetually-courteous Hebrew Clark Kent! Throw away the paintings depicting Jesus as a bland, blonde model for a Breck Shampoo ad!

"You hypocrites!" he barked. Hardly polite words and hardly proper terms for religious leaders. (Not surprisingly, Jesus never again ministered in a synagogue.)

He countered the petty-minded legalism of the synagogue leaders by beating them at their own game. "Does not each of you on the sabbath untie his ox or his ass from the manger, and lead it away to water it?" he demanded (Luke 13:15).

Seeing their affirmative nods, Jesus pinned them. If a farm animal is tied for a few hours, he stated in effect, you show consideration. Why not show the same toward a woman who has been tied for eighteen years? If an animal is worth giving minimal care to, how much more a human? Not only *may* she be released; she *ought* to be! If your religion forbids you from showing basic humanitarianism toward a person, which you show toward an ox or a donkey, something is wrong with your religion!

"Ought not this woman, a daughter of Abraham whom Satan bound for eighteen years, be loosed from this bond on the sabbath day?" Jesus thundered (Luke 13:16).

The woman who had been loosed from being bent stood straight again. "A daughter of Abraham," she reflected, was what Jesus called her. This inspired title conferred a dignity and a status she had never known before. For all of her life—especially during the past eighteen years—she had not even been given the concern or recognition given an ox or an ass. And now, she silently repeated to herself, she was called a "daughter of Abraham" —a beloved member of God's chosen community! She became aware that she was counted one of Abraham's descendants as much as the leaders of the synagogue! She stood taller and straighter than before, conscious of her new standing.

Although puzzled by the way Jesus acted so unconventionally, the woman who had been afflicted with the bad back was one of the first to understand that Jesus insisted on putting compassion ahead of cult, persons ahead of procedures. She knew that Jesus could be highly unorthodox.

The woman healed of her eighteen-year crippling ailment also learned that Jesus' ministry meant tension. Caught in the midst of conflict, she also learned that there can be a creative thrust when Jesus comes up against status quo.

Throughout Jesus' career, there was turmoil. His ministry took place in a turbulent setting. People resisted him.

Significantly, those who resisted him most intensely and provoked the most conflict were the (a) Pharisees, the self-satisfied who resented Jesus' confronting them with their own sin; (b) the pious, the traditionalists who opposed Jesus in the name of their religious traditions; (c) the privileged, the respectable people who held power, prestige, and advantages.

We who feel so guilty, uncomfortable and angry in conflict situations, must remember since Jesus collided with the Pharisees, the pious and the privileged, we will experience conflict any time we challenge any of the same groups today. However, as in Jesus' case there was a positive role for conflict, so with us. Conflict need not be thought of only in a negative sense.

Knowing ourselves and our own blind spots, we realize that we will resist any challenge to our pride and will. Remembering how Jesus' confrontation brought us conflict which resulted in healing and growth, we can sit easy with conflict when we attempt to minister.

And minister we must. Everyone of us has been loosed from crippling infirmities. Knowing something of Jesus Christ, we also know that Christ has released us from the stooped, constricted life-style of seeing only the footprints of our own selfishness. Through Jesus Christ, we are unforgettably aware, God has approached us. He has stretched out his hands in compassion to us who have deserved no compassion. He has healed us so that instead of hobbling helplessly, we can stand up as free women and men. Rejoicing in our newly-given standing and strength, we (like the woman with the eighteen-year infirmity) wish to praise God.

Praising God takes many forms, and many of these forms will bring us into conflict situations. However, around us, a worldful of cripples waits for our hands, our help, our love.

Some are crippled by fears. Others are incapacitated by loneliness. Still others are disabled by guilt. Many are hobbled by grief. Lamentably, all of us are stooped with racism and prejudice.

Countless others are bent over by circumstances and a system which paralyzes—poverty, lack of education, lack of job opportunities.

In the case of the bent-over woman, the synagogue community had been content to give hand-outs to her. They had been inclined to keep her as their pet cripple. Bringing around their baskets at holiday times, the community had felt a little sorry and a little superior. In a way, she was nice to have around because she helped everyone to feel a bit more noble and charitable when they passed the hat for her.

Jesus went further than the rest. He refused to give her aspirin or crutches. Intending for her to be independent, he refused to do anything to perpetuate making her dependent. He meant her to stand as a free person, not to be tethered as a pet to be fed and pitied.

Jesus calls us to be liberators. We, in his name, are to hack loose the forces of evil binding and constricting persons—whether those forces are personal (grief, loneliness, anxiety, guilt, prejudice) or whether they are societal (poverty, homelessness, malnutrition, illiteracy, illness).

Jesus enables us to care—to care in such a way that others may be freed to grow and stand tall like persons. We can risk the conflict that our attempts to bring his kind of healing will produce. But because he has brought release from bondage to us, however, we will reach firmly and joyfully toward others.

THE SEXUAL OBJECT
(Woman of Samaria)

Early each morning while the sun was still low in the sky and the air was cool, the housewives trudged out of the village to the well. Each woman balanced a pottery water jar on her head. Pausing at the well, the women laughed and talked. The ancient well served as a social center for the village wives. Although no woman enjoyed lifting the heavy water jar and carrying it on the long walk to and from the village, everyone enjoyed the small talk at the well. Water-fetching was work, but it was also a break in the monotony of housekeeping. The wives turned the necessary chore into a social event. Each evening, after the oppressive heat declined, the women gathered again at the well to replenish the water supply for their peasant huts. Again, they chattered and gossiped. Every housewife planned her daily routine so that she could join the others at the well twice each day. Like a coffee break for moderns, gathering at the well for the village housewives was a pleasant diversion. Every morning and evening, the women assembled to visit at the well.

It was noon when Jesus and his friends appeared at the old well. They were hot, tired, and hungry after walking all morning.

Glancing at the village, they discussed the fact that they were in Samaritan country. Samaritans and Jews had mutually despised each other for over five hundred years, and Jesus' party wondered whether the Samaritans in the village near the well would even be willing to sell them something to eat. Jesus' friends decided to try to buy food, and hiked into the village.

Sitting on the edge of the well, Jesus waited for them to return. He ran his tongue over his dry lips and looked for some way of getting water from the depths of the well. Realizing that it was the hottest time of the day, Jesus did not expect any of the village housewives to come with a leather bucket, rope and water jar. Parched and weary, he resigned himself to waiting until his friends returned with a few barley cakes, some olives, dates, and perhaps some fruit.

(Jesus was the same as we. He sometimes grew thirsty. He felt tired after a hard, dusty tramp. But he never rustled up a miracle for himself. He insisted on sharing exactly the same conditions and limitations as the rest of us. Although divine, Jesus was also completely human, not a demigod nor a superman.)

Jesus looked up in surprise. He noticed a woman approaching the well with a water jar. At first he was astonished to see a housewife fetching water at high noon. No sensible woman would make the long trip from the village to the well in the peak hours of heat. Besides, Jesus knew that no woman would want to miss socializing with the other women at the well. Jesus sensed immediately that this woman was purposely coming to the well at a time when no one else was about. He surmised that she was trying to avoid meeting other housewives.

Why? He wondered what had caused her to be ostracized. In village life, Jesus remembered, peasant wives were usually a supportive, closely-knit group. Only a few things would cause them to turn against another woman, and suspected immorality always topped the brief list. Jesus deduced that the Samaritan woman had a bad reputation in the village and was deliberately coming to fill her water jar at a time when she would not encounter any other village housewife.

Jesus did a surprising thing: He spoke to the woman, asking her for a drink.

In speaking to her, Jesus smashed three longstanding barriers. First, he spoke to a *woman*—something no Law-observing, self-respecting Jew would do in public (some rabbis even went so far as to refuse to greet their wife or sister in public, and, remember, every devout Jew prayed daily thanking God that he had been born a male).

Second, Jesus spoke to a *Samaritan* woman—a member of a minority group regarded as contemptible compromisers and half-breed heretics. Proper Jews avoided Samaritans, even detouring for miles on a trip to stay away from Samaritan villages.

Third, Jesus spoke to a Samaritan woman of a dubious reputation. No conscientious Jew would consider degrading himself by talking with any woman with the faintest suspicion of a questionable character.

In one quick sentence, Jesus brushed aside all the taboos about conversing with women, with Samaritans and with a person of doubtful morals! "Give me a drink," he asked (John 4:7), doing away with ancient rules fencing off certain persons from God. In one simple human request for a drink, Jesus enacted the searching, smashing desire of God for contact with all outsiders.

Instead of silently handing Jesus the leather bucket and the rope, the Samaritan woman got a bit fresh. She twitted Jesus, a Jew (easily identified by the tassels on his garment), for asking her for a drink. No respectable woman in all Palestine would talk to a stranger, and no self-respecting housewife even in Samaria would speak so impudently to a strange man.

Jesus, however, ignored the banter. Soberly and softly he replied, "If you knew the gift of God, and who it is that is saying to you, 'Give me a drink,' you would have asked him and he would have given you the living water" (John 4:10).

"*Living water!*" The expression meant more than fresh drinking water. Everyone in Samaria, Judea, and Galilee knew that "Living Water" also referred to God. "As a hart longs for flowing streams, so longs my soul for thee, O God. My soul thirsts for God, for the living God" (Psalm 42:1, 2) cried the Psalmist. "Ho, everyone who thirsts, come to the waters," pleaded the writer of Isaiah 55:1. "Living Water" was as common a figure of speech for God, for people in Jesus' time as an expression such as "the Man upstairs" is for us.

The Samaritan woman pretended that she did not understand. Sarcastically, she taunted Jesus. How was he going to get a drink, if he thought he was so great? She snickered as she jibed at the stranger offering her "living water." Who did he think he was—someone greater even than their ancestor Jacob who dug the well centuries ago? Pleased with her smart-mouthed wisecracks, she stood hands-on-hips, boldly confronting Jesus.

Jesus quietly answered that *yes*, he was greater than Jacob. And it was not well water he was talking about, he repeated. Living water, Jesus stated, was what he came to bring. He made it clear that he could offer direction and purpose, peace and joy in life.

Life with him, however, is like finding a deep, inexhaustible artesian well. Jesus made it clear that he brought life-giving refreshment to shrivelled, parched lives.

"Whoever drinks of the water that I shall give him will never thirst," he insisted. "The water that I shall give him will become in him a spring of water welling up to eternal life" (John 4:14).

Perhaps the woman from the Samaritan village was thickheaded. Perhaps she was stubborn—or maybe both. In any case, she was determined not to take Jesus seriously. She insisted on joshing about human thirst.

She interpreted Jesus' words to mean that she would not have to heave around the heavy water jar anymore. "Give me this water," she exclaimed, "that I may not thirst nor come here to draw" (John 4:15).

Shortly after World War I, T. E. Lawrence, the colorful military hero, brought some of his Arab allies to London. The desert sheiks from a water-scarce world were entranced with western plumbing, particularly water faucets from which an apparently endless supply of the life-giving liquid gushed at the twist of the wrist. Returning to the Middle East, many of the Arab warriors carried water faucets home with them in their baggage. Later, Lawrence discovered that his friends expected to have water pour out of the unattached faucets whenever they turned the handle.

With the same obsession for a limitless supply of good water without any inconvenience or effort, the woman from the dry Samaritan village persisted in interpreting Jesus' words with a narrow literalism. "Give me," she greedily demanded.

Living water? Jesus' offer of a spring "welling up to eternal life"? To the coarse Samaritan peasant woman, it sounded like a labor-saving device. She thought only of not having to carry jars and make the long, hot walk to the well. She made it clear that she heard him talking about a modern convenience, a gadget for her comfort.

Like us, the Samaritan woman tried to exploit Jesus. She wanted to "use" God. She tried to take advantage of Jesus. Giggling flirtatiously, she invited him to hook up the fresh spring he had been talking about at her cottage.

Jesus sized her up. He saw this Samaritan woman for what she really was —a shallow, flippant wench of loose morals. He refused to indulge her any further. Abruptly stopping her coquettish come-on, Jesus commanded, "Go, call your husband!" (John 4:16).

Jesus hit the touchiest subject possible for the woman. Mentioning her husband was poking a needle into a raw nerve.

She flinched and stammered, "I have no husband" (John 4:17).

Jesus shrewdly knew that he had probed the sensitive area of her life. However, he did not mumble apologies. He did not smoothly change the subject. Instead, Jesus bore in. With relentless honesty, he pointed out that he could tell that she had lived with some half-dozen men, and that the man she was currently living with was not married to her.

We frequently forget that Jesus brings judgment as well as mercy. God confronts us in Christ with a frank appraisal of ourselves as well as his full acceptance. "And the Word became flesh and dwelt among us, full of grace and truth . . ." (John 1:14)—including the truth about ourselves! We sentimentalize the gospel. We treat God as a sweet, indulgent, senile great aunt in a remote rest home, who rewards our infrequent attention with generous checks and lavish praise.

In Jesus, however, God reveals Himself. He stings us with the truth about ourselves. Jesus "tells it like it is." He does not pussyfoot around. He spills out what we try to hide about ourselves from ourselves and the world.

Jesus exposed all the dark little secrets of the Samaritan woman. Like a giant searchlight, his words focused ruthlessly on the shame she had tried to hide in the shadows for so long.

The Samaritan woman desperately tried to sweep the suddenly-uncovered secrets back into hiding. She could not allow this strange man to show her up for what she was. She and Jesus both knew that she was a cheap tramp who had slept around. But she refused to admit it. Instead of acknowledging her promiscuity and loneliness, she tried to rebuild her pose.

Noting that Jesus was some sort of a religious type, the Samaritan woman nimbly shifted the conversation away from herself. She got Jesus off on a religious topic. "He is a Jew, I am a Samaritan," she thought, "so let's discuss the age-old squabble about whether it's better to worship as the Jews do on Mt. Zion or as the Samaritans do on Mt. Gerizim. That ought to hold him for a while!" She asked Jesus a juicy question about worship customs, dripping with theological, sociological, liturgical and ethical ramifications. Any rabbi would have a heyday, giving a lecture in response to such a question.

Jesus, however, was not sidetracked. He recognized the woman's question for exactly what it was—a dodge. He swiftly demolished both the traditional Samaritan and Jewish arguments trying to localize God on a certain mountain. In fact, he made clear, a new day had dawned. With his coming, all the ancient, worn-out debates about God were now unnecessary. Jesus refused to get hung up on her evasive question.

Jesus, in fact, never philosophized about religion. However enjoyable it may be to hold seminars discussing interesting theological topics, Jesus ignored them. He knew and knows that our petty questions about religion always tend to throw a smokescreen around *the* question, "What is your relationship to God?"

Brushing aside the woman's minor queries, Jesus determinedly tried to confront her with the truth about herself and about him. He wanted her to recognize the new life which he brought.

Desperately she still tried to get Jesus off the topic of her cheap, empty existence. Searching frantically for a safe subject to talk about, the Samaritan woman brightly introduced the matter of the Messiah. Surely, she told herself, this strange man would pick up the scent of this intriguing topic and would stop his annoying habit of bringing the conversation back to her and her life-style.

"I know that Messiah is coming . . ." she jauntily replied, "when he comes, he will show us all things" (John 4:25). *There*, she told herself, that should settle things. At least the conversation was back in a broad, harmless area again. If the strange man wanted to gab some more, he would discourse in generalities about the Messiah. That was fine with her. On the other hand, if he wanted to let the conversation drop, that was all right too. She smiled to herself. Her reference to the Messiah could even be taken as a cue that she was ready to call it a tie and allow each to withdraw without losing face. It had been an awkward encounter for her, but she felt that she had retrieved herself with her generalized comment about knowing all the answers after the Messiah had come. It was a neat close, she thought, and she preened herself over having had the last word. She prepared to fill her water jar, confident that the man would only make a perfunctory reply to her commonplace observation.

Instead, she heard a blockbuster of an announcement.

"I who speak to you am he!" Jesus asserted.

Jesus had had enough of her teasing talk and flippant attitude. He knew that she assumed that she had skipped away by her casual references to the Messiah. "All right, if it's the Messiah she pretends she wants to discuss, I'll call her bluff," Jesus in effect averred. "Perhaps that will bring her around." He openly announced that he was the Messiah! And he did this to a disreputable woman from a despised ethnic minority living in the boondocks!

It seems astonishing that Jesus would disclose his great secret to such an unsavory person. Why would he bother to reveal his identity to a floozy from an obscure, half-caste village? Why didn't Jesus take up her hint that she was willing to close the discussion with her commonplace observations about the Messiah?

Jesus refuses to write off anyone—even Samaritan trollops.

We often mutter that certain others are "not worth it." Why make the effort to become involved with others—especially when they don't appreciate what we do? What's the point, we ask, of knocking yourself out for others who are coarse and unpleasant?

The answer, of course, is simple: God has the same problem with each of us!

We sourly announce that certain ones are not worth our going out on a limb for—forgetting that Jesus has already hung out on a limb literally for them—and for us!

The Samaritan woman was overcome. Knowing that the Messiah had deigned to communicate himself to her in spite of her sordid past, she leaped up and raced down the path toward the village. She forgot her original errand of filling her water jar. In fact, she even left behind her valuable water jar.

"Come!" she shouted to everyone on the streets, "Come, see a man who told me all that I ever did. Can this be the Christ?" (4:29).

She forgot her shame. She freely acknowledged her disreputable past. Moreover, she no longer lived in hiding. Instead of shunning others, she sought them out. Her contact with Jesus meant that all the barriers separating her from God and from others were down. She counted herself a member of the village, of the human race. No more did she have to slink out to the well when no one would see her. No longer did she have to avoid the slurs and glances of the villagers. Her supposedly clandestine affairs were known by everyone and had turned her into a fugitive in her own hometown. Now, however, she could face everyone openly!

Jesus retrieved this dropout from respectable society. He extended her the certainty of his care and acceptance in spite of her miserable character. He released her from her miserable past, he liberated her from her dirty reputation. He gave her a new identity by granting her a glimpse of his identity.

"Got to get it all together," some of our brightest kids cry.

"I don't know who I am, and won't someone give me a clue?"

Answer: Your own sense of personal identity comes when you understand yourself as a person before God. You learn who you are only as you learn who God is. And God discloses His identity through the career, execution, and reappearance of the One who asked the Samaritan woman for a drink one day. Through Jesus the Messiah, the Deliverer or Liberator, you are given your personhood!

THE FUSSER
(Martha)

An ancient monastery clings to Mt. Athos, a rocky promontory on the coast of northern Greece. The monastic community at Mt. Athos claims that it maintains the faith in pure form by forbidding all women. No girls or ladies, even mothers or sisters of monks, have ever been permitted to visit Mt. Athos. So insistent is the stricture against any feminine presence at Mt. Athos that she-goats, cows, hens and all other females are barred!

By contrast, Jesus mixed easily with all persons, female and male. Numerous women were counted among the group of his followers known as "disciples." Although many monastics are secret misogynists, never label Jesus as a woman-hater. He enjoyed the company of women. He felt comfortable in their presence.

In fact, Jesus "adopted" a trio of two sisters and a brother as the nearest thing he could find to a family and home in his manhood. He delighted in visiting Martha, Mary, and Lazarus. Every man yearns for a group where he can take off his shoes and loosen his tie; Jesus found such a haven at Bethany with Martha, Mary, and their brother.

Martha, the older sister, ran the household. Both Martha and Mary delighted in providing the little domestic touches every man needs. Martha, however, always brought a smile to Jesus' mouth by her mother-hen mannerisms. Martha fussed at Jesus because he often did not eat regular meals. She inevitably gave him little lectures on looking after himself. She often chided him for exposing himself to dangers. Both Martha and Jesus knew, of course, that her little scoldings were her own way of expressing her care. Martha's tart tongue belied her warm heart.

"A woman named Martha made him welcome in her home" (Luke 10:38 NEB), indicating the hospitality and kindness which lay behind Martha's friendly reprimands. Martha put herself in the role of everyone's big sister

—Jesus included—and played it to the fullest. When teased about the way she tried to manage everyone, Martha always quipped that she had to look after such silly, helpless babes. And everyone always laughed, including Martha.

One time, however, Martha did not think things were very funny. It was during the Festival of Tabernacles, the big fall harvest holiday commemorating Israel's wilderness wanderings. Each Jewish household built a booth or "tabernacle" out of fresh boughs and celebrated a week-long feast under the ceremonial shelter. Martha, Mary, and Lazarus had constructed their lean-to of green branches. Martha, a take-charge type, had organized the family's celebration, directed the building of their leafy booth, planned menus, supervised the shopping, cooked, and baked. By the time of the feast, Martha was tired.

Just when she was hoping to sit down and catch her breath, Jesus and some friends descended unexpectedly. Martha, pleased to see them, cheerfully offered them hospitality in spite of her tiredness. Instead of letting Jesus and the other drop-ins take potluck with the family, however, Martha thought that she had a reputation as a super hostess she had to keep. She ended by overextending herself.

Through the kitchen door, we could see the scene. Martha hurried from the house to the courtyard, back and forth, back and forth. She lifted the lids of the kitchen pots. She brought fresh water. She calculated the time it would take to serve the main course. She checked the supply of bread. She mentally figured the number of portions of each dish. She wondered if she had enough utensils. She worried if the vegetables were too well cooked. She bustled. She fretted. She rushed around the kitchen. She puttered restlessly with the bowls and jugs under the leafy arbor. She was hot. Her feet were tired and her legs ached. She paused to wipe a strand of hair from her perspiring forehead.

Suddenly, Martha caught a glimpse of Mary, her sister.

Demure and relaxed, Mary had remained with the guests. She sat comfortably in front of Jesus, listening to the conversation. She seemed so idle, so intellectual.

Martha at this point felt just the opposite. Hot, rushed, and disheveled, Martha resented her sister's cool and tidy pose. Martha suddenly boiled with a sense of injustice and self-pity.

Look at her, that little loafer! Martha steamed to herself. *Who does she think she is, reclining there like a princess? We have guests dropping by without warning and it takes all the hands we can find to get a decent meal on the table. What's she doing to help? Nothing! There she sits, as if meals* get prepared and cooked and served by themselves. Meanwhile, I have to work my fingers to the bone! Here I am, with sore feet and a backache. I've got a burn on my hand. And my head is starting to hurt. Trying to get a good dinner for everyone, while that lazy sister of mine takes it easy!

Martha is Mrs. Housewife for all ages. Martha is immortal and international. Dear Martha, wiping her hands on her apron and glancing at her sister in the living room, in the studio, or in the office downtown. Martha notes her own raw hands. By contrast, her sister in the trim lab smock, or in the smartly-styled stewardess mini always appears impeccably manicured and coiffured. Mornings, standing in her faded dressing gown, Martha looks out her kitchen window as Mary languidly strolls to the bus stop. Martha watches her career-girl sister, beautifully dressed and dutifully admired, conversing with the men as the bus approaches to whisk them to places where someone else always does the dishes and sets the table. Martha gazes down at her sink full of greasy plates. She remembers that company is coming for dinner. And the washer is broken and the best tablecloth is dirty. And she's out of sugar and forgot to order rolls from the bakery. Martha grimly purses her lips and stoops to empty the garbage.

Housewife Martha needs to pray daily:

> Lord of all pots and pans and things,
> since I've no time to be
> A saint by doing lovely things
> or watching late with Thee
> Or dreaming in the dawnlight,
> or storming Heaven's gates,
> Make me a saint by getting meals
> And washing up the plates.

Martha of Bethany, tense and tired, fumed to herself. Every time she glanced toward the courtyard, she saw her sister, Mary. Even Mary's pose of calm attentiveness irritated Martha. When Martha caught the whiff of Mary's perfume, she grew angry and jealous. Martha noted the contrast between her sister and herself. The hint of fresh fragrance danced around Mary, while the heavy smell of sweat and vegetables enveloped Martha.

Martha, irked and hurt, made a point of appearing to be even busier than before. She sighed loudly as she trudged ostentatiously through the courtyard among the guests. She cast herself as the overworked housewife. Obviously, Martha was trying to rebuke her sister and embarrass her into getting up and helping.

The ploy failed. Mary continued to stay perched at Jesus' feet with an expression of relaxed enchantment on her pretty face. Tension continued to build. Martha bustled more impatiently than before. A collision was inevitable.

It was time to serve the dinner. By way of summoning her sister to jump up and lend a hand, Martha rattled the plates. No response. Martha repeated the signal with a louder clatter. Mary continued to sit.

That was it! Martha had had enough!

Storming out of the kitchen, Martha strode angrily into the courtyard. She ignored all the courtesies due her guests and her sister. Bristling with indignation, she dressed down both Mary and Jesus.

"Don't you care that my sister has left me to do all the work by myself?" Martha snapped, "Tell her to come and help me!" (Luke 10:40 TEV).

Jesus deserved part of the blame, Martha felt. He had encouraged Mary to abandon her post in the kitchen.

And as for Mary! Martha crackled with such resentment that she could not even bring herself to use Mary's name. Petulantly, Martha referred to Mary as "my sister." Instead of using the proper name, Martha demeaned Mary by reducing her to a common noun.

Martha self-righteously grumped that Mary had been rude and thoughtless. Actually, Martha in the end was *more* rude and thoughtless! Instead of trying to cover for Mary's forgetfulness or instead of using tact to suggest to Mary that she might pitch in and help, Martha reprimanded both her guest and her sister. Martha, losing her self-control, spoiled her own dinner party.

Bossy and authoritarian Martha must make all the decisions. Martha had chosen the menu. Martha had assigned the chores. Martha claimed the right of giving orders to others. Martha assumed command over everyone in her household. Martha further took it upon herself to judge her sister's performance.

Worse than being entangled in busyness was Martha's attempt to entangle others in the same life-style. Martha, resenting her enslavement to her kitchen, wanted Mary to endure the same slavery. Caught herself, Martha determined that her sister would also suffer the fatigue and anxiety.

Jesus retrieved the situation perfectly. Gently, he spoke to Martha. "Martha, Martha," he said, repeating her name to emphasize the affection and concern he felt toward her. Jesus addressed her by name twice to assure her of his undivided attention. Although Martha had belittled Mary by referring to her as an object ("my sister"), Jesus built up Martha by speaking to her as a person with worth and individuality.

"Martha, Martha," Jesus told the breathless woman, "You are anxious and troubled about many things; one thing is needful. Mary has chosen the good portion, which shall not be taken away from her" (Luke 10:41, 42).

Jesus was not praising piety over activism. Nor was he raising prayer over service. There is nothing holier about carrying candles at the altar than carrying trays to a geriatric patient. Nor is there anything more sacred in distributing the wafer at the sacrament than in baking bread for a hungry family. Jesus is not belittling Martha's activism in order to elevate Mary's contemplation. Martha and Mary—each serves. The traits of both sisters are equally necessary. Hands as well as hearts must be present.

In the Age of Consciousness III, there is a trend to downgrade Martha's concern for the practical. Professor John P. Roche of Brandeis recently described how a former student, full of love and enthusiasm, went off last year to a commune. Recently, when the student turned up with haircut, necktie, and no beads, Dr. Roche expressed surprise. The student explained. "The dishes," the youngster said. "No matter how much we rapped about it, nobody would wash the stupid dishes."

Martha rightly knew that *someone* had to do the dishes. And Jesus approved of Martha's down-to-earth realism.

To be devout is not to be indolent. Devotion is not dreaminess. To love is not a license to load. "Vigor and efficiency" are the two characteristic marks of a saint, according to wise old Samuel Johnson.

Even St. Teresa of Avila, the sixteenth century mystic and ascetic, insisted on instilling a healthy dash of Marthaism in her Barefooted Carmelites. (Perhaps she had her hands full with a convent of idealistic young nuns who considered it beneath their dignity to scrub pans or who thought it unspiritual to leave their lofty meditations.) "Believe me," Teresa observed, "Martha and Mary must go together in entertaining our Lord, and in order to have Him always with us, we must treat Him well and provide food for Him. How could Mary have entertained Him in sitting always at His feet if her sister had not helped her? His food is that we should strive in every possible way that souls may be saved and may praise Him."

Jesus always appreciated Martha's hospitality. In fact, he undoubtedly thought of Martha on the morning he had to go without breakfast during the last days of his earthly life. ("In the morning, as he was returning to the city, he was hungry" Matthew 21:18; ". . . when they came from Bethany, he was hungry" Mark 11:12.) Where was Martha? If Jesus had stayed in Bethany, why did he have to go into Jerusalem hungry?

The plot to murder Jesus extended also to Lazarus, Martha's brother, whom Jesus had restored to life. Lazarus, a marked man, obviously had to flee. Undoubtedly, Martha went with Lazarus to look after him. During Jesus' last week before his death, the home at Bethany had no woman to get up and prepare breakfast. Therefore, Jesus had to leave Bethany on an empty stomach. He certainly missed Martha's ministrations in the kitchen.

At the same time, for Martha and all of Jesus' associates, there was both a time to work and a time to listen. On the day at Bethany during the Feast of Booths when Martha lost her cool, Jesus knew that Martha should have taken time to sit and enjoy and be. "Mary has chosen the good portion," Jesus commented (Luke 10:42).

Note that Jesus did not condemn Martha. He realized that her worrying and bustling came from her devotion, but he wanted her to learn to relax and not take herself or her chores so seriously.

Martha thought she kept house, but her house kept her. Instead of holding a dinner party, Martha's dinner party held her.

For Martha, the *et ceteras* took over. Things—the shopping list, the menu, the recipes, the plates and dishes, the schedule, the seating arrangements, the decorations—overwhelmed her. The means of living became the master of her life. Martha became tyrannized by housework.

Jesus the Liberator firmly but gently stated, "Martha, you are anxious and troubled about many things . . ." (10: 41). Martha's agitation and anxiety, Jesus made it plain, were her own doing, not Mary's, not the guests'. Martha had tried to pile on too many activities. Her meal was excessively elaborate. A couple of dishes—even one—would have sufficed.

"One thing is needful," Jesus continued (10: 42). A hospitable heart is what counts, not an exhausting and lavish banquet.

Martha misplaced her perspective. She became so busy that she forgot her reason for being busy: serving Christ. She started well. She decided to show care by feeding. Martha, one of the first activists, realized that social concern is one important (and indispensable) form of ministry. Unfortunately, however, Martha lost the sense of why she was showing this concern.

Worse, Martha became so preoccupied with dinner details that she found no time to sit with Jesus. Result: her efforts quickly lacked their distinctive quality—namely caring. What started as service ended as busywork.

Without time with the Lord, as many modern social activists and other Marthas eventually learn, what begins as a concern of the heart will end as a pain in the back. *Laborare est orare*—"to work is to pray"—runs the old monastic dictum, but Christian monks never claimed that work took the place of prayer. Work, they knew, could be a form of prayer. Work, including social service, results from prayer. Nowhere, however, is work glorified as a substitute for praying.

In our work-oriented culture, most of us are Marthas. We are never too busy to tell how busy we are. We act as if the old Nova Scotia seaman's ditty is an article of faith:

> Six days shalt thou labor and do all thou art able
> And the seventh holystone the deck and scrub the cable.

Our chores as housewives, accountants, clerks or executives too often become an obsession absorbing all our time and energies.

Jesus liberated Martha from the kitchen. He freed her from slavery to a stove.

Work, in the light of Jesus, has no meaning in itself. Work has meaning only when it can be a vehicle for service and creativity. Housework, Martha had to learn, was grinding toil and grim drudgery when she made housework an end in itself. "Any work," correctly stated Martin Luther, "that is not done solely for the purpose of keeping the body under control or of serving one's neighbor, as long as he asks nothing contrary to God, is not good or Christian."

In other words, the kitchen chores are a means of pleasing husband and family!

There is nothing inherently noble about peeling potatoes or stirring saucepans. There is nothing implicitly grand about shoving a sweeper or sewing a seam. A woman will (and should) resent being relegated to the sink and stove as if these were her only rightful places. But when sink and stove can be the means and the setting of caring for others, a housewife will discover that she is liberated from drudgery.

There finally comes a point where every Martha must stop trying to serve and learn to be served. Jesus wanted Martha to catch some of her sister's willingness to receive from him. In her immaturity, Martha tried to work as if she were God. In her insecurity, Martha worked with anxiety and without stopping.

Before Jesus, however, every Martha can understand herself in a new perspective. She (or he, for there are as many males who fuss and worry themselves to the breaking point) can learn to give the gift of *self* to life more generously. "The mature person," Reuel Howe remarks, "is able to work without being a slave and to play without feeling he ought to be working."

When we give ourselves to live more maturely, we give ourselves to our work more joyously. At the same time, we know that we are liberated from slavery to housework or any other kind of job. As freed persons, we are able to distinguish between ourselves and our work.

Before the same liberating Guest, we can separate ourselves from our chores, and with an exuberant sense of release give ourselves to laughing and to loving, to sitting and to celebrating, to dancing and to dining!

THE UNAPPRECIATED
(Mary of Bethany)

The two sisters have completely different personalities. Modern Martha raises vegetables. Modern Mary arranges flowers. Martha types recipes. Mary writes poems. At dusk, Martha closes the windows and turns on the lights. At dusk, Mary sits and gazes at the sunset. Martha wears sensible oxfords. Mary likes to feel the cool grass between her toes. Martha reads her prayers from a book at a set time. Mary sometimes sings impromptu hymns as she strums her guitar.

Not unexpectedly, two such temperaments would occasionally clash. However, Jesus appreciated both Martha and Mary of Bethany. In his visits with the two sisters, he celebrated the diversity between them. He blessed the variety of personalities and sanctified the pluralism of character traits in the home at Bethany.

Each welcomed Jesus to their home in her own distinctive way. Martha prepared elaborate meals; Mary conversed with the Guest. Although Martha on one memorable occasion blew up at Mary for not lending a hand with the dinner, we need not deduce that Mary was a shiftless drone. Possibly she felt that day that everything had been done that really needed to be done. Or, perhaps Mary sensed that she was in Martha's way. Mary, with her reflective and emotional temperament, usually managed to achieve the beautiful balance suggested in the ancient prayer, "O Lord, Thou knowest how busy we must be today. If we forget Thee, do not Thou forget us; for Christ's sake. Amen." (Written by Sir Jacob Astley before the Battle of Edgehill.)

When their brother Lazarus died, each sister mourned in her own way. Mary sat on the floor inside the house, grieving. Martha managed to remain dry-eyed and practical when Jesus came. Always active, Martha leaped up as Jesus approached the house and encountered him outside.

"Why didn't you come when we sent for you? What kept you so long?

Don't you care?" Martha, in effect, demanded. Her words are like sandpaper. "If you had been here, my brother would not have died" (John 11:21).

Jesus immediately sensed that the two sisters thought that he had let them down in their time of need. However, instead of trying to defend himself or explain the delay, Jesus thought of the heartbroken sisters. He quietly reminded Martha, "Your brother will rise again" (John 11:23).

Martha had heard so many conventional condolences during the past few days that she nodded mechanically. Even Jesus' words sounded to her like pious phrases. Martha had heard resurrection talk before. In the official prayers of first century Judaism, the second of the Eighteen Benedictions spoke movingly of resurrection in the ascription, "You, O Lord, are might forever, for you give life to the dead." Martha had choked back the tears when she remembered the hauntingly lovely prayer. Beautiful words, she thought, but pitifully little comfort for someone with the throbbing wound of losing a loved one.

Jesus realized that Martha accepted his words as vague expressions of longing for some wispy future. He knew that she had not understood either what he had said or who he was.

Addressing Martha again, Jesus stated bluntly, "I am the resurrection and I am life. If a man has faith in me, even though he die, he shall come to life; and no one who is alive and has faith shall ever die. Do you believe this?" (John 11:25 NEB).

Martha suddenly saw Jesus from a different perspective. She understood that he claimed to be stronger than death! Doubt and trust struggled within the mind of this practical woman. She remembered the realities of the situation. Her brother's corpse, she knew, had been entombed four days earlier. Yet she heard Jesus insisting that he had the final word—even over Lazarus's dying. Martha blinked and stated an impromptu confession of faith which stands as one of the most profound creeds in history, "I believe," Martha replied to Jesus, "that you are the Christ, the Son of God, he who is coming into the world" (John 11:27).

Immediately, Martha turned and returned to the house. Self-controlled and quietly, she went to Mary, her sister.

Mary, distraught and disheveled, sat crying on the floor in the midst of the overturned benches and chairs. During the first week of the thirty-day mourning period, it was customary for the bereaved to give vent to grief by upsetting the furniture and sitting mournfully without washing their faces or combing their hair. Mary, the demonstrative sister, kept the customs.

When Mary heard that Jesus was asking for her, she got up and went out, followed by the group of friends who were trying to console her.

Mary saw Jesus and collapsed at his feet in a paroxysm of crying. Unlike the tightly-controlled Martha, Mary wailed uncontrollably. Between sobs, she blubbered the same words Martha had said, "If you had been here, my brother would not have died" (11:32). Obviously, Mary and her sister had told each other this thought previously. Mary, hurt and bewildered, forgot her usual poise before Jesus. Grief made her chide Jesus. Mary agreed with Martha that Jesus had let them down. When they had asked him to come, he had delayed. Now, it was too late. Hopeless. Mary heaved and shuddered with crying.

"I talk of quiet and hush, and I praise concentration, but I rush about like a dervish and act as though the life here below were a mad dash from x to y—two unknown points," Quaker mystic Rufus Jones once wrote to his wife. The words could have been written by Mary at the time of Lazarus's death. Losing her reflective calm as the poetess who liked to sit at Jesus' feet instead of serving the meal, Mary cried and berated Jesus. In spite of all of the God talk Mary had soaked up, life seemed to be merely a mad dash between two unknown points.

Significantly, Jesus' reaction was not to preach a sermon or tell Mary to pull herself together. Instead, he wept. The Greek word means that the tears rolled down his cheeks.

"Jesus wept" (11:35). This is the shortest verse in the entire Bible. It is also one of the most meaningful. The words suggest that God is not an unfeeling robot. Nor does He stand in icy detachment. Rather, He cries with us. Unlike the Greek Stoics' divinity, whose main characteristic was inability to feel any emotion, Jesus began to cry with Mary. Our God shares our tears.

At the same time, He is not helpless. Through Jesus Christ, He demonstrated conclusively His authority even over the grave.

Jesus, who had announced, "I am the resurrection and I am life," proceeded to put content into his words. Moved with the deepest emotions, he walked to Lazarus's tomb. "Take away the stone," he ordered.

Everyone gasped.

Practical and outspoken Martha was the only one to speak. "Lord," she bluntly stated, "by this time there will be an odor, for he has been dead four days" (11:39). Martha articulated what everyone knew, namely, that the ghastly sight and sickening smell of a putrifying corpse would greet them.

Part of Jewish folklore was that decay started on the fourth day after death as the drop of gall which had dripped from the angel's sword causing death began to work its effect. The rabbis taught that the spirit remained near the body for three days, but after that there was no hope of resurrection. *The Tradition of Ben Kaphra*, in fact, stated, "Grief reaches its height on the third day. For three days, the spirit hovers about the tomb, if perchance it may return to the body. But when it sees the fashion of the countenance changed, it retires and abandons the body."

Mary had not heard Jesus say anything about raising Lazarus. In fact, she had not even heard Jesus' words, "I am the resurrection and I am life." She appreciated Jesus' comfort. After all, tears can be a form of communication. However, after all was said and done, Mary believed Death was still the stronger and still the greater reality.

At Jesus' insistence, some mourners rolled the heavy cartwheel-size stone along its groove to one side, exposing the three-foot square opening to the tomb.

Jesus shouted, "Lazarus, come out!" (11:43). (Interestingly, the Greek word for "he shouted" is used only eight times in the New Testament. Six of these times are in John's Gospel, and four of John's six times describe the shouts of the crowd to have Jesus crucified. The crowd's shout brought death to Jesus, but Jesus' shout brought life to Lazarus!)

Jesus called forth Lazarus from death. He gave back a brother to Mary and Martha. More important, he gave them—and us—a sign of his power over the worst adversary of all—Death. And what was hinted at that day by a tomb at Bethany was spoken clearly and completely when Jesus himself was brought back from Death's grip. Jesus' own resurrection clarified and completed the message stated through the raising of Mary's brother.

Astonishingly, the narrative closes abruptly. The gospel account does not feature interviews with Lazarus about what it was like after he died. No one wrote down what Mary or Martha heard from Lazarus after he stumbled out of the tomb that day. Everyone obviously wished to emphasize Jesus Christ. Lazarus's raising, Mary, Martha, Lazarus, and the gospel writers would have us understand, was simply a sign pointing to him who stands vital and powerful as the resurrection and life.

Mary, the emotional poetess, had long sensed that Jesus accepted her and appreciated her when no one else would. Mary often felt inadequate. Her older sister scolded her. Others criticized her for her sentimentalism and her sensitivity. Jesus, Mary knew, was the one person who understood that she enjoyed conversing with him. Mary felt grateful that Jesus did not insist that her place was in the kitchen, as everyone else did. Mary felt a sense of self-worth whenever she talked with Jesus. She believed Jesus to be an extraordinary person. Who else could liberate her from her sense of being such a cypher, a nothing?

After Jesus restored Lazarus to life, Mary felt a still deeper sense of gratitude for Jesus. Furthermore, Mary intuitively grasped that Jesus was more than merely another mortal human. With the inspired insight of an artist, Mary became aware that Jesus was God's Chosen.

Mary wished to express both her guess about Jesus and her gratitude to Jesus. How could she make objective what was essentially something subjective? In the twentieth century, Mary might have written lyrics or sculpted. She might have donned a leotard or composed. In the first century, however, Mary could not turn loose her artistic temperament. In fact, in Mary's time, it was seriously debated in the schools whether or not a woman had a soul at all!

Thwarted, lonely, misunderstood, Mary longed for some means to communicate her appreciation for being appreciated by Jesus. Time became a critical factor. The noose was closing around Jesus, Mary shrewdly observed. Bethany, just over the hill from Jerusalem, buzzed with rumors how Jesus would be seized. Would there be any opportunity to demonstrate her feelings? Mary wondered. She dared not discuss what was in her heart with Martha. Mary knew that Martha would not understand. Besides, Mary had had enough of Martha's tongue-lashings.

One day, word came to the sisters' cottage that Jesus was approaching. Quickly, Martha and Mary prepared to welcome him. They busily swept the house, shopped for extra food and started to fix a meal for their guest and his friends.

As Mary overheard the conversation, she became aware that Jesus believed that he would live only a short time. Others listened but did not hear what Mary heard. Mary shook with fright. Jesus was going to die—soon. She noted that no one seemed to understand this fact, not even his closest associates. Mary observed also that no one really seemed to care when Jesus announced his imminent death.

Mary, however, comprehended what no one else could. Jesus would have to lay down his life. Mary understood all the awful importance of his words.

In a few hours, Mary knew, Jesus would be gone—for good. How could she explain what she longed to express to him?

Impulsively, Mary rummaged through her few possessions. She could lay her hands on only one thing of value—a jar of ointment.

Some ointments, processed from the gummy resin from a low balsam-like shrub in central south Arabia and northern Somaliland formed the base for incense, cosmetics, perfume, medicines and burial preparations. Other ointments were prepared from a plant raised on the hills near the banks of the Ganges in distant India. Because these essences were so costly, they frequently were diluted with oil or mixed with cheaper balsam gum. Carried into the bazaars in the Middle East, the substance was poured into narrow-necked jars to avoid spilling and to permit only one drop to escape at a time through the tiny opening.

Mary's little jar contained pure, undiluted ointment—the most expensive kind. Even the jar carved from alabaster, required a considerable outlay. Jar and contents were fantastically high-priced, costing three hundred denarii. One denarius equalled a good day's pay for an average working man; therefore, Mary's alabaster jar and ointment represented an investment of a man's total wages for about one year.

Nearly all of Mary's life-savings were tied up in that jar. Because it was the high-priced stuff, she was obviously saving it for her own burial-anointing. A decent funeral with proper anointing was not an extravagance but a matter of propriety. Sensitive Mary, who had lived with criticism and scorn most of her life, had resolved that when she died no one would belittle her. She had carefully saved for the vial of ointment for years, and had secretly hoarded it among her few personal possessions.

The minutes were slipping away and Jesus' visit would soon conclude. Mary made an immediate decision. She would use her precious ointment to anoint Jesus.

Seizing the small alabaster flask, Mary rushed into the room where Jesus reclined, eating and chatting with the other guests. Instead of shaking out a drop or two, telling herself that this would do, Mary threw away caution and forgot all prudence. She recklessly broke the narrow neck of the expensive bottle so that the contents would empty all at once. Before the eyes of the startled guests, Mary applied the costly ointment on Jesus.

No one had ever seen such lavishness. As Mary cheerfully shook the ointment on Jesus in extravagant generosity, the men began to murmur. The rich, exotic fragance reached out to every nostril, delighting yet disturbing the guests.

Just like a woman, they thought. *Clumsy, impulsive, and wasteful, dumping an entire jar of expensive ointment on someone, and even smashing the jar in the process,* the men snorted. With their village-shopkeeper minds, these men who had crowned arithmetic the queen of the sciences quickly calculated the value of Mary's act. These guests measured and hoarded everything. They even shared love only by parcelling it out in tiny pinches. They prided themselves on being rational and reasonable, practical and prudent. These men always knew to the penny what their bank balances were. Their world was wallet-sized.

When they saw a woman uncalculatingly pour out her fortune in one passionate, spontaneous act, they felt threatened. Unconsciously, they sensed if this sort of thing caught on, their own buttoned-down feelings would begin to show and they would no longer be allowed to measure their caring. Normally cool and controlled, they peevishly denounced Mary. They huffed, indignantly, "Why was the ointment thus wasted?" (Mark 14:4). Why was it not given to the poor? Why this silly womanly gesture? Why?

In a sense, Mary's act *was* a woman's act. Mary cared without computing the cost. Nearly every woman understands this. Most women understand Mary's exuberant, extravagant kind of caring. Mary's lavish, straight-from-the-heart concern for her friends appeals. Jesus instantly surmised this truth about Mary.

When he heard grumblers finding fault with Mary, Jesus replied, "Let her alone; why do you trouble her? She has done a beautiful thing to me . . . She has done what she could" (Mark 14:6–8).

Mary picked up whatever she could lay her hands on and showed her commitment joyously and generously. It was not how much or how little it cost at the market. Mary had seized the opportunity to care when it was at hand.

Mary had the satisfaction of knowing that she had broken open the alabaster jar of caring while Jesus was still with her. Nicodemus, who also broke open a supply of expensive ointments, waited until Jesus was dead (see John 19:39). Unlike Nicodemus, Mary never had to berate herself for holding off until it was too late. Mary had the happy knack of pouring out the fragrant ointment of love at the right time.

How few of us have this sense of timing. Most of us timidly and stingily refuse to break open the alabaster vase of caring—and regret it later.

Dyspeptic Scottish minister-author, Thomas Carlyle was such a man. Grim and critical, he spared few words of kindness on Jane, his wife. After her death, realizing how he had failed to use the opportunities of expressing his love for her while she was alive, he wept bitterly, "Oh if I could see her face once more, were it but for five minutes, to let her know that I always loved her through it all. She never did know—never!"

Mary, however, "had done what she could." And Jesus accepted her act not because either Mary or her deed was perfect. Mary wasn't. And the act was clumsy. But Jesus saw the motive. In spite of the limitations and imperfections, Jesus accepted both gift and giver.

Every perceptive parent understands this. When a smiling, grimy-faced little boy rushes in, clutching an already-wilted bouquet of crushed dandelions in his dirty hand, and offers them as a present to his mother, mother (perhaps inclined to throw them out) places the drab weeds in a vase to grace the table for dinner. Taking a cue from Jesus, a parent appreciates what lies behind the present.

After her gift of anointing Jesus was accepted, Mary no longer felt inadequate. Esteemed by Jesus, she felt an esteem for herself. She became aware that Jesus freed her from worrying about censure and scolding by others. Mary rejoiced at being permitted by Jesus to express her care even in impulsive, offbeat ways. Mary was liberated from stewing about what the neighbors would say, liberated from fretting over Martha's criticisms. Her blithe, sunny, artistic temperament and reflective creativity, she happily sensed, were unshackled. Gone was the guilt because she couldn't cook a meal like Martha. Gone was the uneasiness and half-regrets that she wasn't a housekeeper like other women. Thanks to Jesus, Mary knew she could hum, and relax with friends, and admit that she had feelings, and sometimes have a good cry, and laugh, and occasionally do kooky things, and show oceans of care—all without remorse!

Jesus releases an exuberant spontaneity in those who live for others. Life, with him, is no longer all dull prose but takes on a lilt of poetry.

The epitaph of a certain bishop buried in Exeter Cathedral reads, "He was a stern foe to all enthusiasm in religion." Not so with Jesus! Mary discovered that the Liberator unleashes a radiant enthusiasm in both liturgy and living!

Jesus did not sentimentalize Mary's gift. No spray-it-with-cologne-and-the-whole-world-smells-sweet ideas here! Rather, he added, "She has anointed my body beforehand for burying" (Mark 14:8).

Knowing that his death was near, Jesus said, in effect, that his body was ready for the funeral, embalmed in the most beautiful way of all—by the love of a friend. An act done in the spirit of Mary's impulsive and generous care was the best kind of burial preparation he could want. Mary's gesture was the true form of anointing his body for entombment. Jesus stated that he could die in peace because at least one person—Mary—had caught his kind of sacrificial concern for others! His vibrations of caring for others had prompted her to grab whatever was at hand to show love!

"And truly, I say to you," Jesus added, "wherever the gospel is preached in the whole world, what she has done will be told in memory of her" (14:9).

"A good name smells sweeter than the finest ointment" (Ecclesiastes 7:1 NEB). "The fragrance of a good perfume spreads from the bedroom to the dining room; so does a good name spread from one end of the world to the other" (The Midrash Rabbah on Ecclesiastes 7:1).

Mary's name will always have the pleasant aroma of lavish, unconstrained caring.

So does anyone's name who begins to respond to *the* Name. Because of that Name who permitted His body to be broken and blood to be spilled for us, you and I will exhibit a break-the-alabaster-jar and pour-it-all-out passion to care for others.

THE EXECUTIVE'S WIFE
(Joanna)

When Joanna married Chuza, she dreamed of happy, comfortable years together. True, it was a mixed marriage. She was Jewish, and he was Nabatean, from the Arabian peninsula.

Many of Joanna's old friends disapproved of the match. Not proper for a good Jewish girl to marry outside the faith, they said.

Joanna told herself that they were simply jealous. After all, look what she had as Chuza's wife! Most young Jewish brides, Joanna thought smugly, were struggling to make ends meet as the wives of poor Jewish farmers, shepherds, and craftsmen.

Chuza, on the other hand, served as Herod Antipas's chief steward. The title meant that Chuza was business manager and general superintendent of all Herod Antipas's enterprises. Herod's business activities, investments, and real estate holdings demanded outstanding administrative and financial skills on the part of Chuza.

In addition, Herod had a compulsion to build. Perhaps it was to emulate his father, Herod the Great, who had made a name for himself for his grandiose palaces and the impressive temple in Jerusalem. Herod Antipas determined to leave his mark also as a builder. His territory, of course, was only one-third as large as his father's, because Herod the Great's kingdom had been carved into three chunks when the old man died, and Herod Antipas's part included only Galilee and Perea. Herod Antipas resolved to turn Galilee and Perea into a showplace. He began to build.

More correctly, Herod gave the orders to build. Translating these ambitious ideas to reality fell on Chuza's shoulders. Chuza had the heavy responsibility of doing all the planning, organizing, financing, and general overseeing.

Thanks to Chuza's considerable skills as a good executive, Herod Antipas's dreams began to take shape. Tiberius, Herod's capital along the Sea of Galilee, began to assume proportions of being an impressive little Greek-Roman metropolis.

Joanna had not liked the idea of building the capital at Tiberius. She knew that the city was being built on the alleged site of an ancient cemetery, and therefore situated on an "unclean" location. She mentioned her reservations about placing the city in an unclean area, but got no response from her husband. Chuza, not being Jewish, she reminded herself, simply could not understand.

Besides, Chuza was busy. His responsibilities were immense, but fortunately his title of chief steward gave him the power and the prestige to match the responsibilities.

Chuza's competence and accomplishments did not go unrewarded, in other ways, either. He became a moderately wealthy man.

At first, Joanna liked the publicity and attention of being Chuza's wife. She noticed, with delight and satisfaction, that attendants respectfully opened doors and servants were eagerly attentive when Mrs. Chuza approached. Joanna also enjoyed the luxuries which Chuza's comfortable income afforded them. Sometimes, she smiled and wished that her Jewish friends could see her in her role as the wife of Herod's chief steward. She could imagine their envy and surprise.

As Tiberius grew, Joanna noticed, however, that Herod's capital grew more lavish and his retinue seemed to grow more lascivious. She heard the reports of Herod's lewd parties at the spa just to the south of Tiberius. Whenever Chuza mentioned that he, too, planned to soak in the warm spring-fed baths, Joanna tried to protest. To a girl raised on the strict sex ethic of Judaism, it seemed to be an offense even to visit such a place.

Joanna could never shake off her heritage as one of the chosen. Her very name, *Joanna*, meaning "God is gracious," served as a constant reminder of her unique relationship to Yahweh and His people.

Although devoted to Chuza her husband, she found herself thinking that the man she had married seemed to be such a stranger. Chuza, she noted, never seemed to want to understand her or her background as a Jew. She wondered sometimes what this haughty man, a proud descendant of desert warrior tribesmen and traders, was thinking.

Joanna also pondered the fact that Herod Antipas, in spite of his Jewish ancestry, had lapsed completely from the faith of his fathers. She secretly despised the way in which Herod on suitable occasions would parade his Jewish-ness to impress the populace or important visitors. With her intimate knowledge of court life, however, Joanna knew what a sham Herod's religion was.

Would her own offspring end up this way? Joanna worried. The free-floating hedonism of Herod's court seemed to pervade and pervert everything and everyone.

Joanna began to sense the aching loneliness of not belonging. Herod's entire entourage was foreign. Herod's wife, daughter of Aretas, a powerful Arab chieftain, was also Nabatean, and her bevy of friends and personal staff was mostly Arabian. No matter how gracious Joanna tried to be, she felt that she was an outsider.

When it became an open secret that Herod, always a playboy, had become involved in an affair with Herodias, Joanna felt disgusted.

To begin with, Joanna knew that both Herod and Herodias were already married. Furthermore, even if not, the relationship would be forbidden because they were close relatives. Joanna also had heard of Herodias's notorious string of dalliances with other men and her two incestuous marriages, first to her stepbrother, and presently to Philip, her uncle. Joanna could never trust the beautiful, ambitious Herodias.

Inevitably, news of the notorious affair leaked out. Herod's Jewish subjects were shocked. Already affronted by reports of the high living and loose morals in Herod's court, every Jew in the realm felt affronted by Herod's latest escapade.

Joanna watched nervously. When Herod's wife, enraged at her husband's flagrant infidelity, packed up and returned to Aretas, her father, Joanna waited with deep anxiety. She had been married to a Nabatean long enough to know the deep sense of personal honor bred into every Arab. Joanna, aware that Herod's queen's family would feel deeply insulted, knew that Aretas, Herod's father-in-law, would brood and plot to avenge the slap.

Herod, preoccupied with his mistress Herodias, ignored the threat and made plans to marry Herodias. Chuza, walking the tightrope of not showing any pro-Nabatean sympathies and appearing to be totally loyal to Herod, brought his frustrations and tensions home. He, too, knew that Aretas would insist on retaliating for the way Herod had spurned his daughter. The sultry heat of Tiberius, Joanna told herself, was nothing to the torrid pressures building up in the country.

Like a *khamsin*, one of the intense and terrible sandstorms sweeping out of the desert, Aretas's desert fighters suddenly rushed out of the Transjordan Mountains, galloped across the valley wasteland and attacked. Although Herod and Herodias, their personal retainers and staff including Chuza and his family all escaped the onslaught, Herod's forces were routed. Aretas's warriors surged through Tiberius, looting and vandalizing, and left.

Joanna hoped that the humiliating defeat might make Herod mend his ways. Instead, she quickly saw that the episode merely made Herod more touchy and tyrannical.

When Herod went ahead with his plans to marry Herodias, Joanna felt repulsed by the vulgar pomp. After Herod's wedding, Joanna tried to avoid the palace as much as possible. As Chuza's wife, she had to put in an appearance on ceremonial occasions for her husband's sake. Joanna detested the giggling, whispering sycophants who seemed to populate Herod's court. Although she was not invited to Herod's frequent parties, knowing what drunken orgies they were, she despised them.

Joanna began to feel more out of place as Herodias and her nubile daughter (by her first husband), Salome, swished around the capital. Joanna believed the rumors that Herodias could get Herod to do anything she wanted by wheedling or pouting. Sometimes, she felt ill after being in the presence of some of Chuza's business associates and their wives for a time, and, furthermore, she was bored.

Chuza, engrossed with tending to Herod's business affairs, had little time for Joanna or home. Sometimes, his work would keep him busy for several days without a break. When he returned to their house, he was so tired and preoccupied with his work that he offered Joanna little sympathy in her bouts of illness.

Although various physicians prescribed tonics and treatments for Joanna's elusive ailments, she continued to feel vaguely afflicted. She heard that a spellbinding preacher named John the Baptizer was attracting immense crowds to the south in the Jordan valley. Joanna toyed with going to hear John the Baptizer in the hope that some religion might make her feel better. However, when she heard how John the Baptizer was denouncing Herod and Herodias for their illicit behavior, Joanna thought better of it. She did not want to put Chuza in an embarrassing position by attending John the Baptizer's revival meetings.

Joanna found herself mesmerized by the accounts of John the Baptizer's preaching. Secretly gleeful at the way he thundered against the royal marriage, she privately cheered him on. At the same time, she noted with apprehension that Herodias had also heard about the Baptizer. Joanna, acquainted with Herodias's temper when crossed, sensed that the queen would quickly come up with a devious scheme to silence John the Baptizer.

John the Baptizer, meanwhile, continued his biting sermons and became the talk of the kingdom. Thundering dire warnings against anyone—royalty included—who refused to repent and recognize God's rule, he inevitably incurred the wrath of Herodias and Herod.

Joanna gasped when she heard the news that John the Baptizer had been seized by Herod's secret police and hurled into a dungeon in Herod's grim Machaerus fortress. Her malady returned, and she felt sick for days. She knew that Herodias had hounded the king to clap John the Baptizer into prison. Joanna suspected that Herodias would also try to engineer John the Baptizer's execution.

When John continued to languish in his cell deep in Machaerus, Joanna told herself that perhaps Herod would ultimately show clemency and release John, in spite of Herodias's plotting and pushing to have John murdered. She listened intently to the rumors of messages smuggled out of John the Baptizer's cell and to the reports of previous public speeches. God's new age, Joanna understood from these reports about John's preaching, was about to come and the hour of judgment was upon Israel. Another, however, was to follow him who would usher in the new era, Joanna heard. Who was this deliverer who was to come? Joanna wondered.

Suddenly, with the flash and crunch of the executioner's axe, John the Baptizer's voice was stilled. The terrifying abrupt finality of John's being beheaded and the events leading up to it made Joanna swoon and collapse.

One of the first to hear the details of the night of John the Baptizer's death, Joanna learned that Herod and his cronies had held a wild, drunken blast at Machaerus. Usually, these were stag affairs, but Herodias had managed to crash the party. When Herod and the boys had imbibed freely and had their powers of resistance and judgment lowered, Herodias cunningly sprung her surprise. Salome, Herodias's daughter, pranced out and entertained Herod with a dance with such erotic, suggestive movements that the lustful old fool recklessly offered the girl anything she desired. Herodias, lurking in the wings, groomed her daughter to demand John the Baptizer's head on a platter. Minutes later, gory and dripping blood, the preacher's severed head, fresh from the executioner's block, was paraded around the hall amidst cheers and laughter.

Joanna, weak and ailing, could find no medication to bring her relief. She wondered whether anyone could make her feel well again.

People, she heard, were talking about a rabbi from Nazareth who was healing people in Capernaum. Joanna listened eagerly to the reports. Some people, she learned, said that this rabbi, Jesus, was the one promised by John the Baptizer.

Capernaum lay a few miles to the north of Tiberius, and Joanna decided to seek out the teacher-healer named Jesus. She had deep misgivings whether Jesus would consent to see her. Joanna remembered that she was a woman, and recalled her girlhood training about rabbis never conversing with women. Joanna also considered the fact that she was married to Chuza, one of Herod's most trusted aides. She wondered whether her marriage to a non-Jew and to a non-Jew deeply involved in Herod's government would disqualify her from seeing Jesus. Joanna knew that the many scandals of Herod's court had deeply offended pious Jews. Would Jesus consider her guilty by association?

Her anxieties proved to be unnecessary. She discovered that Jesus had no inhibitions about talking with her, a woman. Nor did she find that he applied labels to women because of the husband's backgrounds or positions.

Joanna met other women who, like herself, had come to Jesus for help. She felt reassured that she was not alone or strange.

Best of all, Joanna was granted healing from the nagging infirmities which had been debilitating her. Jesus had liberated her from the ennui and free-floating anxiety of middle years.

Joanna began to walk the five miles to Capernaum every morning to listen to Jesus. Also some women who had been healed of evil spirits and infirmities: "Mary, called Magdalene, from whom seven demons had gone out, and Joanna, the wife of Chuza, Herod's steward, and Susanna, and many others, who provided for them out of their means" (Luke 8:3) joined the coterie of learners (disciples) around Jesus. Because Jesus and the group of twelve he was training as fellow preacher-healers had no income, Joanna and some of the other women with means cheerfully contributed money for food. Joanna and the other women, having few responsibilities at home, joined the group each morning or occasionally stayed overnight with friends. When Jesus began his preaching tour throughout the cities and villages of Galilee, "preaching and bring the good news of the kingdom of God" (8:1), Joanna joyfully accompanied the group.

At the same time, Joanna was frightened. Herod and Herodias, Joanna knew, had also heard about Jesus. Their effective intelligence apparatus, Joanna was aware, kept them well informed about what Jesus said and did.

At first, Joanna noticed warily, Herod reacted superstitiously. She observed that the king took seriously the swirling rumors about Jesus, especially the weird ones, such as Jesus being John the Baptizer revivified, or Elijah or one of Israel's ancient prophets risen from the dead. Joanna learned from authoritative palace sources that Herod was particularly troubled by the whispering that Jesus was John the Baptizer returned to life.

Later, Joanna heard through the palace grapevine that Herod, because of Herodias's prodding, not only had Jesus under constant surveillance but was making plans to arrest Jesus.

Joanna, thoroughly alarmed, fleetingly wondered about her own safety. She hoped that being the wife of Chuza, one of Herod's most indispensable assistants, would shield her.

More important to Joanna was Jesus' security. She quickly sought him out, and warned him that he was in desperate danger in Herod's territory. She learned that others, including some Pharisees who had not been friendly toward Jesus, but even less friendly toward Herod, had also urged Jesus, "Get away from here, for Herod wants to kill you" (Luke 13:31). Joanna smiled when she heard Jesus refer to Herod as "that fox"—the only time in which Jesus ever dubbed a human with the name of an animal.

Although Joanna felt relieved when Jesus got out of Herod's kingdom, she worried about Jesus' future. Joanna, like many others, had found herself wondering about Jesus' identity. Preacher-healer-prophet extraordinary, to be sure; but Joanna and everyone in Jesus' movement suspected that he was more. Some whispered that Jesus was the long-awaited Messiah, God's promised Deliverer.

Joanna waited restlessly for additional reports of Jesus. She sensed the growing tensions in Galilee as well as in Herod's household about Jesus. When Joanna heard that Jesus intended to carry his message to Jerusalem at Passover, she knew that Jesus meant to confront the leaders of Israel with his announcement that, through him, God's new age had arrived.

Fortuitously, Herod announced that he and his retinue would also journey to Jerusalem for Passover, and Joanna knew that she could accompany Chuza and be in the Holy City at the time when Jesus would appear. She sensed that the situation was ominous for Jesus.

In spite of the rousing welcome given Jesus by Passover pilgrims, Joanna knew that plots against Jesus were proliferating. She wondered why Jesus had decided to expose himself to the risks of coming to Jerusalem.

Her fears proved correct. Although Joanna was asleep in her comfortable quarters when Jesus was snared by the temple police, she heard at breakfast the details of the trumped-up charges, the illegal nighttime hearing before the Sanhedrin, the early morning arraignment before Pilate and the appearance before Herod. Joanna did not need to be told that Herod and his bullies treated Jesus "with contempt, and mocked him" (Luke 23:11).

Hurriedly, Joanna sought out some of the other women followers of Jesus. She, Mary Magdalene; Salome, Mary the Mother of Jesus, and other women gleaned what reports they could. Jesus, they heard finally, was sentenced to die by crucifixion.

Joanna gasped. She had vivid memories of crucified victims. Galilee, always boiling with revolt, had been treated literally thousands of times to the ghastly sight of men shrieking in pain and gasping for breath, eyes bulging and tongues protruding in gruesome death grimaces. Joanna needed no explanations of what lay in store for Jesus. She wept.

Bravely determined to be with Jesus and the other mourning women, Joanna forced herself to go to Golgotha, the place of execution. She endured the nightmare-experience of witnessing the murder of Jesus and two minor guerilla leaders.

Ravaged by grief, emotional exhaustion, and despair, Joanna stumbled back to Jerusalem. She and the other women agreed to meet at the tomb at dawn as soon as the Sabbath, due to begin at sunset, was over. Joanna planned to contribute some expensive ointment to place around Jesus' corpse as a sign of respect for his memory.

Instead of finding the grey body of a dead Jesus, however, Joanna and the other women discovered that the tomb was empty. They were astonished to hear a report that Jesus had been raised to life again. Hurrying back to Jerusalem, they reported the announcement to the other disciples. Joanna sighed when the men dismissed the women's report as "an idle tale" (24:11).

Shortly afterward, Joanna, the other women as well as the men followers, experienced the most liberating life-drama in their own histories as well as in world history: Jesus Christ was alive!

The news that God had raised Jesus from the tomb still enlivens and emancipates modern-day Joannas.

Drifting in a crisis of purposelessness? Wife of an executive, does life mean little more than face-lifts, hair tints, quack diets, quack religion, and forever gazing over a sea of bridge tables? Medicine chest starting to look like a drugstore because of hypochondriac ailments?

Walter Lippman, speaking of many contemporary women, says that she "has emancipated herself from the tyranny of fathers, husbands, and homes, and, with the intermittent but expensive help of a psychoanalyst, is now enduring liberty as an interior decorator."

"*Enduring* liberty"—an apt description of much which results from current Lib efforts.

Real liberty begins when one is freed from being obsessed with *self*. All attempts to find freedom which emphasize self produce greater slavery. Their slogans may grow more shrill. All efforts, however, which are rooted in self-aggrandizement are doomed. Personal Lib starts with crucifixion of self. Resurrection-freedom is given by God, not attained by human tries.

"If any man [or woman] would come after me, let him [or her] deny himself and take up his cross and follow me. For whoever would save his life will lose it, and whoever loses his life for my sake will find it." The Risen Lord persistently reminds the Joannas and Chuzas of every generation with these words from Matthew 16:24, 25.

THE SOCIALITE
(Pilate's Wife)

A haughty Roman patrician to her bejewelled fingertips, Claudia Procula was used to power and privilege. After all, she was a member of the illustrious Claudius clan, one of Rome's "first families," and could trace her ancestry to the earliest days of the Republic. Claudia Procula had been raised, like members of the former ruling class in Britain or old wealthy families in America, with an awareness of her station and destiny as one of the nobility. She had been nurtured on stories of members of the Claudius family—a distinguished line of statesmen, generals, poets, orators and builders (one had constructed the famous Appian Way)—and their services to Rome.

Claudia Procula also had been exposed to the decadence and debauchery of upper-class Rome. When she was in her teens, in A.D. 14, a close relative, Tiberius, one of the famous Claudius family, was proclaimed Emperor. Although the tough old warrior was such a severe disciplinarian that the men from his own legions mutinied when they heard of his succession as Emperor, Claudia Procula and everyone in her circles knew that he could not—or would not—control his own family. The scandalous conduct of Julia, Tiberius's only daughter, raised even the eyebrows of the blasé Romans. The Queen Mother, Livia, wove a tangled skein of intrigue and plots. Agrippina, the Empress, winked at all moral aberrations.

When a young army officer named Pontius Pilate was posted to Tiberius's household, Claudia Procula noticed that at least one member of the imperial staff did not seem obsessed with orgies, perversion, and promiscuity. She enjoyed his stories of campaigns against the German tribes. She admired his ambition. Although years later, Agrippa, a Palestinian puppet-king, correctly called Pilate "inflexible, merciless, and obstinate," in her palmier days Claudia Procula saw these same character traits in a complimentary light, and felt he had "will, character, and strength." Young

Claudia Procula was impressed that Pilate was a man who "won't be pushed around," who "knows his own mind," who "forms his own opinions," and who "knows where he's going."

Although Pilate did not have Claudia Procula's bluestocking background, he was a good marriage catch. He counted himself a member of the equestrian (upper middle-class) order. To get into the equestrian class in Roman society took either money (at least 400,000 sesterces) or pull with the emperor—and usually a combination of both. Pilate also held a prefecture, a coveted commission either putting him in charge of an auxiliary cohort or a wing of cavalry, or permitting him to serve as a legionary tribunate of the second class (first class open only to those in the Roman senatorial order).

Claudia Procula accepted Pilate's marriage proposal.

She soon felt uneasy about the way her husband persisted in trying to ingratiate himself into favor with Sejanus, Emperor Tiberius's most trusted advisor. Claudia Procula had watched Sejanus's rise to power with uneasiness and fascination.

Starting as a prefect of the praetorians, Lucius Aelius Sejanus cleverly buttered up Tiberius until he became virtual ruler of Rome. Sejanus, a suspicious and treacherous tyrant, instituted political prosecutions. Buttressed with an elaborate web of informers and spies, Sejanus had hundreds seized and executed on the slightest suspicion of treason. He convinced the Emperor that suspected rivals within the imperial household had to be eliminated, and even managed to poison Tiberius's own son, Drusus, Tiberius's daughter-in-law, Agrippina, and her two sons, before Tiberius finally woke up to Sejanus's evil designs. Sejanus was finally executed in A.D. 31 after ruling in effect as joint emperor for years.

Claudia Procula recognized Sejanus's administrative skills and dictatorial powers. However, she grew increasingly unhappy as Pilate, her husband, was drawn into Sejanus's orbit of associates. She noted that Pilate began to acquire many of Sejanus's mannerisms and attitudes. For example, when Pilate began diatribes against Jews, Claudia Procula observed that he was displaying the same venomous anti-Semitism and even using the phrases for which Sejanus was famous. Secretly, Claudia Procula became alarmed. She sensed that Pilate's relationship with Sejanus was coarsening him. Pilate, she noticed, began to show more of an ugly side to his nature.

She commented about his increasing animosity toward Jews, his unbridled ambition to push to the top, his participation in the intrigue of the Roman court. Pilate indignantly replied that it was the way to get ahead. Claudia Procula told Pilate that he seemed to be changing, that he appeared to be imitating Sejanus. They argued. Claudia Procula suddenly saw that the man she had married had turned out to be an arrogant, cunning adversary instead of a sensitive, compassionate lover.

She wept. He swore, made perfunctory apologies, and assumed that everything would be all right.

The relationship, Caludia Procula knew, would never again be the same. She resented Sejanus's vicious influence. Like a malignant tumor, Sejanus's evil ways seemed to have taken root in her husband's life. Claudia Procula thought to herself, "If only we could get out of Rome, and live some place where Pilate will not feel compelled to be a toady to Sejanus and his henchmen."

Claudia Procula and Pilate quarreled frequently. Between arguments, she observed, there were short-lived, grim truces. Somehow, they did not seem to be able to recover the old relationship.

It began to occur to Claudia Procula that everything about Rome—the dizzying round of exciting court intrigues, the dazzling spectacles in the circuses, the sumptuous feasts and holidays—seemed inane and tiring. Were these vices and pleasures all there was to life? She sometimes thought that some religion might help. When she remembered the official state cult, with its veneration of her aloof relative, Tiberius, with his scandal-ridden household, she quickly passed to the next on the list. The old Greek and Roman mythologies, with their gods and goddesses cavorting shamefully, were a tired joke to Claudia Procula and her class. She knew that many of her husband's army friends practiced Mithraism, a popular cult attracting thousands, who submitted to the messy, secret ceremonies involving the blood of bulls and extolling virility. Claudia Procula, a refined and cultured person, felt disgusted. She also rejected the Greek mystery religions, with their stress on esoteric knowledge and elaborate rites for the favored initiates.

What about the Jews? Claudia Procula wondered. She had heard of their high idea of The One God, of their stubborn rejection of sexual permissiveness. At the same time, she remembered Pilate's sneers against everything Jewish. Someday, she told herself, she would learn more about what they taught.

Meanwhile, Claudia Procula felt her marriage and her life in idle Roman high society growing more empty.

She listened dutifully as Pilate described his wire-pulling to get himself an appointment in government service as a procurator. She knew that he was the right age, for a procurator had to be at least twenty-seven to thirty years old. She also remembered that Pilate had the necessary prerequisites for the job, namely service as a prefect or tribune. Knowing the labyrinthine ways of Roman political appointments, however, Claudia Procula was aware that her husband would also need to have his cause advanced by someone with political clout. For some time, she recalled with disgust, Pilate had been cultivating Sejanus. When she discovered that Pilate was also exploiting her family ties with Tiberius, Claudia Procula was irritated at first. She resented the shameless way her husband was angling for a promotion, even by trading on her family connections. At the same time, Claudia Procula grudgingly admitted that his scheme just might succeed. And if it succeeded, she remembered, Pilate would be transferred out of Rome.

A transfer! Claudia Procula daydreamed about the possibility. She even found herself wondering about locations. Would it be an appointment to a pleasant, throbbing city like Alexandria? Or a cultured capital like Athens? An exotic location on the lovely Dalmatian coast?

The dreamed for announcement finally came through. Pilate received his coveted appointment as a Roman procurator. The couple celebrated with an elaborate banquet with their friends. Meanwhile, they anxiously waited word on where Pilate was to be assigned.

When Pilate and Claudia Procula heard that Pilate had been appointed procurator over part of the Roman province of Syria, to a cluster of eastern Mediterranean hill-satrapies called Judea, Samaria, and Idumea, they were crestfallen. The procuratorship of Judea, Samaria, and Idumea was not one of the plums in the Roman foreign service. In fact, it had the reputation of being one of the lowest rungs.

Claudia Procula tried to cheer her husband by pointing out that Judea, Samaria, and Idumea could be just the first step toward bigger and better things. If he did a competent job, she assured him, he would be promoted.

Secretly, however, Claudia Procula suspected that Sejanus, Tiberius and the other important people of Rome had reviewed Pilate's dossier, and had detected the same flaws she had observed. She even wondered whether they were playing some sort of weird joke on Pilate by posting him, with his outspoken anti-Semitic views, to the place where Jewish culture was strongest. Deep inside, Claudia Procula felt a premonition of trouble ahead for her husband. She knew his loathing of Jews, his brusque army manners, his quick temper, his tyrannical nature. Some sort of collision, she sensed, would result.

Originally, Roman magistrates were not allowed to take their wives to the provinces. Emperor Augustus even had a law passed forbidding wives to accompany provincial governors. By A.D. 26, however, when Pilate received his appointment, the old law was being ignored. Tiberius permitted government officials to take their wives as long as the husband guaranteed that the wife would not interfere in state affairs. In fact, Tiberius required his appointees to post special security to prevent their wives from involving themselves in their husbands' work, and provided stiff penalties for any wife caught interfering in imperial business.

Pilate and Claudia Procula made the long journey from Rome to the eastern Mediterranean in A.D. 26. They settled in the luxurious official residence, formerly one of Herod's palaces, in the town of Caesarea. Claudia Procula's womanly appreciation of beauty was captured by the magnificent view of the azure sea and the picturesque shoreline.

Coming from the highest social rank, Claudia Procula had previously had little personal contact with Jewish culture. She had been attracted by what she had heard. Coming to the land of the Jewish God, His prophets and His people, made her more curious. Through a slave girl, she bought a translation of some of the Jewish scriptures. She had never read anything like them. She quickly noticed that they lacked the graceful superficiality of the dilettante philosophers and orators. Claudia Procula, however, felt drawn to the raw, unadorned message of The Eternal One and His dealings with His chosen.

As soon as Pilate and Claudia Procula arrived in the province, Pilate immersed himself in his job. He had little time for his wife. Pilate commanded three thousand Roman troopers at Caesarea, numerous small garrisons strategically located throughout Judea, Samaria and Idumea, and a cohort of five hundred soldiers in the chief trouble spot, Jerusalem. His main responsibility was to serve as chief administrator of the tax system for the imperial treasury. With his troops as a constant reminder that the country was under control of the Roman occupation army, Pilate had to make sure the cash kept flowing to Rome.

Pilate also was the supreme judicial authority (except in cases of Roman citizens) in Judea, Samaria, and Idumea. Roman policy was fairly enlightened, allowing a large degree of self-government in occupied areas. In Palestine, the Romans had permitted the Jews to retain their own high court, the Sanhedrin, to prosecute and try their own cases. Except for the death penalty—which required the procurator's approval—the Romans kept hands off the Jewish courts. Pilate, at least in theory, should have been able to work out a fairly comfortable working relationship with the Jewish authorities.

Claudia Procula watched her husband with trepidation. She knew his contempt for the Jews. On their first trip up to Jerusalem from Caesarea, she saw how he bristled when he did not find Roman standards, banners of other visible reminders of the imperial presence in Jerusalem. Pilate grew incensed when he learned that Roman insignia was never brought into Jerusalem because of deference to Jewish sensibilities. Claudia Procula looked at the determined but unruffled Jewish leaders. As her husband fumed and swore, she noted the contrast between him and men so secure in their faith that they could face the representative of the most powerful empire in the world without flinching. She wondered what emboldened these Jews.

Claudia Procula soon learned that her husband was determined not to make the least effort to accommodate himself to the Jewish population. She heard him give the order as soon as they returned to Caesarea to have a strong detachment of troops march into Jerusalem by night, bearing the Roman standards with the Roman Emperor's insignia. "It's time to show these Jews who's in charge" Claudia Procula heard her husband telling one of his aides.

Two days later, Claudia Procula was wakened by shouting outside. She lay in bed, wondering what was causing what sounded like the roar of an angry crowd outside the palace. She finally slipped to the window. When she looked out through the lattice work of her window, she shrank back in fright. Thousands of enraged Jews, a heaving sea of humanity, filled the area around the residence and spilled into the streets of Caesarea. She shuddered as she heard their furious protests about the hated insignia in Jerusalem.

Claudia Procula quickly dressed and ran to the part of the building Pilate used as his headquarters. She found him perspiring nervously and issuing a stream of commands to his staff, ordering the Jews to disperse at once.

Hours later, when the courtyard still had not emptied and the crowd turned more hostile, Pilate angrily spat out a warning, "Tell the Jews to clear out or I'll have to use force."

The crowd remained. Irate, Pilate sent out an ultimatum. The demand: that the Jews break up and leave immediately, or he would turn loose his legionnaires with instructions to kill.

Not a Jew moved. Tension mounted. The crowd sullenly waited, taunting Pilate to carry out his grisly threat. Toughened troopers buckled on their swords. Officers looked at Pilate, waiting for the next order.

Nervously, Pilate tapped his fingers. He knew that he dared not unleash his troops. The news of the massacre would reach Rome, and his career would instantly end. He cursed angrily, and asked his aide whether the Jews had started to leave. Hearing that they had not, he tried to appear confident.

Claudia Procula and everyone present, however, knew that the Jews were calling Pilate's bluff. In spite of her husband's loud assurance that the Jews would leave by sundown, Claudia Procula sensed that he knew that he would have to back down. No one in the room had had more exposure to Pilate's petulance and wrath than Procula. The long-suffering woman correctly predicted that he would pace the floor in fury and fulminate against the Jews for half the night.

Next morning, to Claudia Procula's surprise, she woke to find that the crowd had still not dispersed. She found it difficult to believe Pilate's forecast that hunger and thirst would force the thousands outside to disband by noon. She had studied some of the faces of the Jews squatting in the palace area, and sensed a flinty stubbornness. What kind of devotion to what kind of God did these people have?

The third and fourth days passed, and the sullen crowd of thousands of Jews remained camped in Caesarea. Finally, on the fifth day, Pilate sent for the ringleaders. They parleyed, and Pilate agreed to remove the despised Roman standards from Jerusalem.

Claudia Procula had a new depth of understanding and appreciation for the Jews. She realized that her husband, however, had only deeper loathing for them. Months later, she also saw that Pilate had learned nothing from his encounter in Caesarea.

Pilate stupidly commanded that a number of gilded votive shields inscribed with Emperor Tiberius's name be hung in the Holy City. Again, the Jewish population erupted in angry demonstrations. Pilate stubbornly refused to yield. Reports of the tumult got to Rome. This time Pilate received orders from Tiberius himself to remove the shields immediately and also a stern warning not to repeat that kind of nonsense.

Claudia Procula felt uneasy, knowing that her husband was on probation. She longed to help him in some way. Every time she suggested showing some sensitivity toward the Jews, however, she received an angry rebuff. Claudia Procula, in turn, quietly began to delve more into the traditions and the faith of the Jews.

Claudia Procula also hoped that Pilate had learned his lesson. Instead, to her dismay, the notorious disturbance over the water system broke out.

Pilate, determined to improve the insufficient Jerusalem water supply, planned to build an aqueduct. To finance the construction costs, he high-handedly decided to dip into the temple treasury. Predictably, the Jewish leaders were incensed. Another ugly mob scene followed. Pilate sent soldiers disguised as civilians to mingle with the crowd. On signal the soldiers suddenly began bludgeoning everyone, including women and children, brutally but effectively clearing the streets. After this episode, Pilate was thoroughly hated by every Jew in Jerusalem.

Claudia Procula, meanwhile, was finding deep satisfaction in Judaism. Her thirsty soul discovered the springs of refreshment in the story of Yahweh's promise to His people. She saturated herself in the story. She longed to identify more closely with the people of that promise. Although both her background and her position as the Roman procurator's wife meant that she could never be accepted as a Jew or call herself a Jew, Claudia Procula became a "proselyte of the gate." This was as near as a Roman could come to embracing Judaism, and was a step taken by numerous thoughtful and devout Romans who like Claudia Procula felt drawn to the profound monotheism and high ethical demands of Judaism. For anyone who was not born a Jew, becoming a "proselyte of the gate" was the next best thing. Claudia Procula, a devoted proselyte, continued to study Torah, began to pray regularly, started to give alms and to observe the Jewish festivals. Although she did not mean to conceal her affiliation with Judaism, Claudia Procula took pains to be discreet about it before Pilate. She knew his irrational enmity toward the Jews.

During the second year of Pilate's ten-year stint as procurator of Judea, Samaria, and Idumea (he was finally ordered home in disgrace to stand trial in A.D. 36) while Claudia Procula was quietly immersing herself in Judaism, she began to hear reports of a certain Galilean rabbi named Jesus. Claudia Procula was curious about Jesus. She heard conflicting reports. Some snickered that this Jesus was just a hillbilly preacher. Others whispered that there were rumors that he was the long-promised Messiah. Everybody admitted that Jesus' preaching and healing created the biggest stir in Galilee since Judas the Galilean's revolt twenty years earlier.

Claudia Procula had heard enough reports about Galilee to know that it was considered to be the hotbed of insurrection. Pilate, she remembered, constantly received word about plots and attempted uprisings in Galilee. She had seen large numbers of political prisoners from Galilee—hot-eyed rebels calling themselves the Zealots—who infiltrated across the borders into Pilate's area to stir up trouble and got themselves arrested. Although Galilee was not under Pilate's jurisdiction (to his intense disgust, Rome allowed a playboy wastrel named King Herod Antipas to look after Galilee) Claudia Procula knew that Galilee and its fiery revolutionaries caused her husband constant trouble. The garrisons bordering Galilee were regularly dragging down to Caesarea or Jerusalem batches of Galilean guerillas in chains and under heavy guard.

Claudia Procula wondered whether this Jesus was not another Galilean insurrectionist. After all, she reminded herself, she had heard that he frequently talked about a new kingdom. Many in Galilee, according to authoritative reports to her husband, wanted to crown him and have him lead a great new uprising against the detested Roman occupation forces.

Although she felt drawn to Judaism and prayed, gave alms, and tried to keep the Law, Claudia Procula could never forget that she was a Roman. As a Roman, she realized that she would forever be an intruder in Judea, Samaria, and Idumea. She acknowledged to herself that to Jews she would always be one of the enemy.

This Galilean named Jesus, she told herself, probably despised her. Undoubtedly he, too, would reject her as a hated Roman, the wife of the top man in the occupation army.

With a shudder, Claudia Procula recalled that her husband and his fellow Roman officers had never been known for their gentleness in Galilee. In fact, she remembered the war stories of campaigns against Galileans told at officers' parties. One that stuck in her mind was how the Romans quelled the Galileans' revolt under Judas the Galilean by publicly crucifying two thousand Galileans. Claudia Procula grimaced when she thought of two thousand boys and men, groaning and writhing from the agony of being spiked to upright posts and left to die. Reluctantly, the woman admitted, the Romans' crucifixions of Galileans was bound to breed counteratrocities. For all their vaunted civilization, Claudia Procula recognized that her fellow Romans could descend to unspeakable levels of barbarity.

Pilate's wife thought sometimes of Rome. In spite of occasional mild homesickness over not seeing family and friends, she sensed that she no longer belonged in Rome. She could never again endure the vacuous round of boisterous parties. She had no yen for the busy intrigue of court life. And yet, Claudia Procula knew that she could never belong to Judaism. In short, Pilate's wife was a spiritual orphan. She had no real home. Claudia Procula could never be accepted either as a Roman or as a Jew. When she brooded on the situation, she often felt depressed and lonely. Sometimes her sleep was troubled with strange dreams, reflecting the uneasy emotional state she was in.

Four years passed from the time when she and Pilate arrived in Caesarea. Their marriage had wilted. Pilate, assertive and reckless as always, neglected Claudia Procula to administer his territory. Claudia Procula, her beauty.

fading, felt the encroaching desolation of the start of middle age.

When Jewish Passover time approached for the fourth time since they had moved to Palestine, Claudia Procula wearily prepared to pack and move to Jerusalem for two weeks. Passovers were always crisis periods for Pilate, and Claudia Procula had deep apprehensions. This year particularly, she knew, tensions had been mounting in Jerusalem. Rumors and reports of Jesus the Galilean coming to Jerusalem at Passover time had been brought to Pilate's attention. Jerusalem, always simmering with unrest, could blow up when thousands of Passover pilgrims, fired to fever pitch with nationalism, poured into the Holy City. Although Claudia Procula intended to observe the Jewish commemoration of the ancient episode under Moses in her own way, she did not relish what might break out in Jersualem during the coming weeks. The political situation, she shrewdly observed, was so volatile that anything could happen. And knowing her husband, she dreaded what he might do.

Riding up the twisting road from the coast, Claudia Procula looked with awe at the splendor of the ancient city's location, perched on the skyline of the high Judean ridge. She smiled as they rode past groups of Jewish pilgrims, chanting their *Hallels* as they approached the Holy City for Passover.

After a two-day journey from Caesarea, she, Pilate and their retinue settled themselves in the impressive palace built by the great King Herod. Claudia Procula, however, was not comfortable. Her psychic antennae picked up messages that the political pressures and psychological strains of the Jews in Jerusalem had grown more intense. With a sense of foreboding, Claudia Procula prepared to have her own private version of Passover.

A few days before the actual Day of Passover, she was startled to hear the sounds of a great disturbance. Claudia Procula nervously rushed to her window to peer out. A huge crowd was surging through the gate near the temple. Fortunately, the crowd seemed orderly and the sounds were happy and peaceful. Everyone seemed elated about the arrival of a man riding a donkey at the head of the procession. Claudia Procula heard the cheers, "Hosanna! Hosanna! Blessed is he who comes in the name of the Lord!" Branches and cloaks, she saw, were tossed in the pathway of the man on the donkey as a sign of homage.

Suddenly, it became clear to Claudia Procula that the Jewish populace was acclaiming the man on the donkey as the Messiah! She also noticed that none of the Romans understood this. The Roman officers and Pilate's staff looked on the procession with amusement and contempt, joking with each other about the natives' parades. As long as the crowd was not menacing, the Romans ignored it.

The biggest surprise, for Claudia Procula, however, came when she learned that the man being cheered was Jesus, the rabbi from Galilee. So this was the famous Jesus who had stirred everyone so deeply, Claudia Procula thought. The only Roman woman in the gospel accounts and the only woman of high social rank to be affected by Jesus took a long look—and wondered.

Years later, after she and her husband had been forced to return to Rome after his ordering innocent, unarmed Samaritans slaughtered on Mt. Gerizim and she and Pilate were banished in disgrace, Claudia Procula often recalled the Passover when Jesus came to Jerusalem. Claudia Procula remembered how fascinated she became with this strange Galilean.

He had not been the firebrand she had previously thought he would be. He was a revolutionary all right, but she discovered that his program was not so much directed against Rome as it was for a commitment to God's rule. Claudia Procula was disconcerted by the way Jesus assumed that he was inaugurating a new age of God's rule.

She never forgot the occasion when Jesus was dragged before her husband. The night before, she had been unable to get to sleep, wondering about Jesus. She had eventually drifted off, but slept fitfully. During the night, she experienced a vivid dream about Jesus. She woke trembling and crying. Deeply shaken by her dream about Jesus, she laid awake the rest of the night thinking about him. Normally in control of herself, Claudia Procula found herself frightened and uneasy. Her stomach felt tight, and she was gripped by a nameless premonition of horror.

When the sun finally rose, it was the day before Passover. Jerusalem seemed electrically tense. Suddenly, she heard a commotion outside the palace. A noisy collection of courtroom types and temple police were banging on the gate and demanding to see Pilate immediately. Peeking, Claudia Procula put her hand to her mouth in surprise. Below, chained to guards, stood Jesus.

She heard the gate creak open and the group of police and accusers troop into the main hall. Calling her maid, Claudia Procula commanded her to find out what had happened.

Shortly, Claudia Procula learned that Jesus had been too threatening even to the Jewish leaders. The Galilean leader had been seized during the night and tried by an irregular gathering of the Sanhedrin. Pronounced guilty of blasphemy, Jesus was slated to die. Under the Romans, however,

Jesus could not be executed by the Sanhedrin without permission of the Roman procurator. Therefore, the Galilean rabbi was dumped before Pilate.

To speed the case along, however, and to make the case more impressive, Jesus' accusers changed the charges when they appeared before Pilate. They knew that Pilate would respond better if he heard that the prisoner was trying to overthrow Rome. Instead of blasphemy, therefore, they yelled that Jesus was guilty of treason.

Claudia Procula, knowing how surly Pilate was before breakfast and how contemptuous he was in the presence of Jews, expected him to turn them all out.

Instead, he grumpily climbed into the judgment seat and called for order. Claudia Procula realized that Pilate dared not ignore the charges. The horde shouted that Jesus advocated sedition. This was a grave matter, and Pilate, who was in disfavor with the home office, knew that he could not stand to make another mistake.

Claudia Procula studied the defendant. Never, even in the imperial court, had she ever encountered such majestic bearing. She heard the phrase, "King of the Jews," flung at Jesus, and she commented to herself that truly he conducted himself better than any king or emperor. What a contrast between him, she thought, and the shrieking rabble of paid informers, police, assorted goons and toughs, petty politicians and curiosity-seekers who had crowded into her husband's courtroom. And what a contrast between Jesus and her husband, the embodiment of imperial might. It seemed to Claudia that Jesus embodied divine might. Without question, she told herself, Jesus dominated the scene.

Strangely, however, Jesus refused to testify in his defense. With icy calm, he politely declined to refute the charges.

Pilate, mystified, tried to prod him to answer. When the prisoner continued to stand silently, Pilate grew irritated.

Claudia Procula, knowing well the mannerisms of her husband, recognized the telltale signs of Pilate's mounting exasperation. She sensed that he would dispose of the case in one way or another as soon as possible. When he was angry and hungry, she knew that he became more abrupt. She began to suspect that her husband might acquiesce to having Jesus executed.

The horror of having Jesus put to death swept like a cold blast over Pilate's wife. She shook and tried to fight back tears. Her dream of the night before suddenly came back to her. Crucifying this Galilean seemed to

Claudia Procula to be the worst injustice of the ages. And to think that her husband might be party to the deed!

Struggling to get hold of herself, Claudia Procula immediately decided to take a drastic step: to interfere with an official Roman judicial process!

Roman jurisprudence, still the foundation for most western nations' laws, was a majestic and orderly legal system and permitted a surprisingly equitable administration of justice. Under no circumstances were women—especially wives of magistrates—to meddle in the courtroom. If the wife or any relative of a Roman magistrate presiding at a case interfered in any way, they were automatically guilty of contempt of court and subject to severe punishment.

Claudia Procula, who had been surrounded with the Roman system since infancy and who knew the theory and practice of Roman law better than most citizens, was aware of the desperate consequences of the step she took.

She sent a message to Pilate.

"Have nothing to do with that righteous man, for I have suffered much over him today in a dream" (Matthew 27:19), she pleaded.

Claudia Procula risked anything—even censure, fine or imprisonment—to rescue her husband and Jesus.

Pilate was jolted. He realized what lay behind the message. He knew the danger Claudia Procula was going through to send the message. Never before had she interfered in his magisterial affairs. He recognized that his wife considered this situation an emergency. "She must think it's urgent that I release this Jew from Galilee," Pilate grasped. Pilate pondered the situation.

Wringing her hands in the doorway, Pilate's wife waited. *If this Jesus were to die, he would die because of my husband and me,* she thought. And she wished that somehow she could be forgiven.

As she watched, her husband vacillated. She could tell that he knew that Jesus was innocent. She also sensed that the crowd realized that Pilate was equivocating. She heard their cries grow more shrill and insistent. To Claudia Procula's dismay, Pilate weakly asked, "What shall I do with Jesus who is called the Christ?"

Yes, thought Claudia Procula, *what shall anyone do with Jesus? That's Pilate's question—and mine, too!* (In fact, that is *the* question of life. Commitment or crucifixion, which will it be? Ultimately, what you and I do with Jesus will lead to one or the other.)

"What shall I do with Jesus who is called the Christ?" Claudia Procula made up her mind what she would do with Jesus who is called the Christ;

according to tradition, she became a convert. She is even hallowed in the Greek church as a saint, and honored on October 27 on the Greek church calendar.

Her husband Pilate finally caved in to the pressures and permitted the death sentence to be carried out.

Jesus died because of Pilate and me, Claudia Procula reminded herself. Later, however, she learned to change the words from "died because of" to *Jesus died for Pilate and me.* Through Christ's crucifixion, she became aware that God forgave even a Roman woman of rank!

THE NEUROTIC
(Mary Magdalene)

Early in 1971, Israeli scholars announced the discovery of the skeleton of a man crucified about 2,000 years ago. The skeleton, found in a cave tomb in the outskirts of the northeastern sector of Jerusalem, had its heel bones pierced by a seven-inch iron nail. Experts who examined the bones stated that the victim, of average height and stature, was a young man probably in his late twenties at the time of his death. Detailed archaeological evidence indicated that the young man died from crucifixion early in the Christian era.

All scholars, Christian and Jewish, hastened to state that it was absurd to suppose that the bones were the remains of Jesus. Anthropologists and anatomists pointed out that it was impossible to identify any skeletal remains with Jesus because we have absolutely no knowledge of Jesus' physical stature. Historians and archaeologists add that crucifixion was such a common method of execution—involving thousands in the ancient world—that it was preposterous to relate this skeleton to Jesus.

In spite of the testimony of these learned experts, however, some gullible souls seized on the announcement and tried to link the skeleton to Jesus Christ. Those who suggested that the bones belonged to Jesus apparently were, like the women on the first Easter, still expecting to find Jesus' corpse. These pathetic people, one must infer, have never been surprised with the resurrection announcement.

A woman named Mary Magdalene was the first who went to the tomb, intending to identify his body by the nails through the hands and heels. Mary Magdalene knew exactly where to look; she had been an eyewitness to his death and the removal of his body. Although it must have been a sickeningly ghastly sight, Mary Magdalene had watched everything, even the final journey when the corpse was deposited in the tomb. She and the other women had marked the tomb's location carefully.

"Mary Magdalene and the other Mary were there, sitting opposite the sepulchre" (Matthew 27:61). Totally weary, the two women could no longer stand.

Mary Magdalene's future? Everything in her life had been bound up in the message and career of Jesus. With him dead, Mary's purpose and plans had died. What next? Trudge back to Magdala?

Mary *Magdalene:* carrying that name was almost like wearing an ugly facial tattoo. Mary the Magdalene (always with the article whenever she is mentioned in the New Testament) hailed from Magdala on the west shore of the Sea of Galilee, and people from Magdala never boasted of this fact, especially among proper Jews.

Magdala, the hub for trade routes converging from the hills and lake, bustled with commerce and industry. Its boatyards, fish-curing racks and warehouses made it a center of wealth in Galilee. Because most of the population was Gentile, the wealth brought a taste for some of the unsavory pleasures of the Roman world. In fact, the very name, *Magdala,* could refer to one who plaits her hair—the term used for women of questionable morals—or could refer to a tower or fort. In the first century, Magdala even had its own hippodrome for entertainment, to the disgust of the nearby Jewish population. The city carried an evil reputation. Later, the rabbis claimed that Magdala fell because of its wickedness.

Wealth and immorality have a Satanically destructive effect. Although we have no way of knowing, these might have been two of the seven "demons" afflicting Mary the Magdalene at one time.

We do know that Mary of Magdala once suffered from being possessed by demons. Although we react with a smile of superiority at the mention of demons, to the ancients they were real. Demons were the forces of evil infesting the universe, the agents of illness and emotional disturbance. In Jesus' time, all superhuman terrors and all powers thwarting God's will were labeled "unclean spirits" or demons. Studies in psychosomatic medicine make abundantly clear that, although the terminology of the first-century world may sound strange, there are nonorganic, nonphysical causes to many of the illnesses of many patients today. Even now we speak of the "spirit of defeat" or "bad emotional climate" as if these were malign forces at work. Whatever medical diagnosis we may wish to give to Mary of Magdala, we can be certain that, as a demon-possessed woman, she was indeed a seriously ill patient.

So ill, in fact, that she was described as having been gripped by seven demons. Seven demons meant that Mary the Magdalene's condition was desperate. Only those who were afflicted with recurring attacks and locked in a state of hopeless immobility could be classified as strait-jacketed by seven demons.

As Mary Magdalene sat bleakly facing the tomb where Jesus' mangled, bleeding corpse had been laid, the demons of grief and bewilderment, self-pity and anxiety, loneliness and bitterness, and a host of other virulently malevolent forces tore at her.

On another occasion, when Mary Magdalene had been so manacled by seven demons, Jesus had liberated her from their pernicious grip. Passing through Magdala on his way to Capernaum, Jesus had answered the appeals to help the hopeless case.

Mary, set free by Jesus from thralldom to her evil spirits, committed herself to serving Jesus as wholeheartedly as she had given over her life to her private demons. Mary of Magdala felt free at last. No longer did she feel captured by nameless terrors. No more was she possessed by powers of destruction and death.

A person of some substance, Mary the Magdalene gratefully shared her money with Jesus and the Twelve. She, Susanna, Joanna (the wife of Herod's steward) and others realized that neither Jesus nor his disciple band had any savings or investments and provided enough financial support to feed them.

With others of Jesus' followers, Mary the Magdalene had journeyed to Jerusalem that fateful Passover. They all had come, expecting their charismatic leader to announce clearly his destiny as Israel's Deliverer, yet fearing that he might come to harm. Their worst fears were realized. Jesus was seized. Hours later, he hung on a cross.

He had cared about others and had cared about society so much that he had torn away all their delusions. He tried to give the world a new consciousness of what God meant life to be. He had exorcised the demons of anxiety, guilt, anger, and futility. For his efforts, he was not dismissed as a nuisance but executed as Public Enemy Number One. No genial gentleman, Jesus posed such a threat that people responded either violently negatively or partisanly positively. He provoked either execution or exorcism. People either had to let him destroy their bondage to personal and societal demons, or they had to destroy him. Jesus demanded rugged Either/Or responses; he put everyone through Life/Death showdowns.

The earliest grey of dawn had just begun to appear over the distant Moab hills when Mary Magdalene and a few others roused themselves. During the thirty-six hours since Mary of Magdala had left Jesus' tomb, she and the other women had grieved together, waiting out the Sabbath. Rest—

the purpose of Sabbath—eluded them. After sunset marked the end of Sabbath, legally permitting them to visit the tomb, darkness followed so soon that they knew they would have to wait until daybreak and return to the tomb. Although physically and emotionally drained, few slept for long during the second night after Jesus' death. Tensions had been too high. And just as they had finally settled into a restless doze, they had been disturbed by tremors of a predawn earthquake. Drawing their shawls around them to keep warm, Mary the Magdalene and her companions gathered up the spices with which they intended to anoint Jesus' corpse. They padded through the dark and empty alleys, slipped through a little-used passageway in the city wall, past snoring guards, and moved silently toward the burial place. Their black head-shawls and garments made them almost invisible in the murky darkness.

Mary the Magdalene's main concern was how she and others would manage to work aside the enormous circular stone slab sealing the entrance to Jesus' tomb. To move such an enormous disc, she remembered, usually required a squad of men with heavy poles to pry and hefty shoulders to push. She wondered whether they might persuade the Roman guard to help them move the stone.

Through the mists and darkness, the little party of grave visitors approached the tomb. They descended the steep steps chopped out of the limestone face. They looked around for the guard, but could not see him. They moved toward the entrance of the cave. Instead of finding the stone still in place with Pilate's seal unbroken, however, they saw that the stone had been rolled to one side. Astonished and upset, the women rushed to the opening and peered inside.

The tomb was empty! Jesus' corpse was missing.

The women were startled to see a young man sitting on the right side, just inside the entrance.

"Don't be alarmed," he said. "You are looking for Jesus of Nazareth, who was nailed to the cross. But he is not here—he has risen! Look, here is the place where they laid him. Now go and give this message to his disciples, including Peter: 'He is going to Galilee ahead of you; there you will see him, just as he told you' " (Mark 16:6, 7 TEV).

The shaken women rushed up the steps, up the trail, along the road, through the gate and across the city to where Peter and a few of the Twelve were holed up. Banging on the door, they finally roused the men and told them the astonishing message. Mary Magdalene and the others noticed that the men looked at them skeptically. The report, Mary Magdala acknowledged to herself, sounded dubious. Crucified men, she and everyone present knew, did not rise from the dead.

Disconsolately, Mary of Magdala drifted back toward the tomb.

The pressures of the preceding days had been nearly overwhelming. That morning, finding the body missing and hearing an impossible announcement, Mary's emotional reserves were exhausted. She broke down and cried.

She was wailing so hard she did not notice the Stranger. Through her sobs, she barely heard the question, "Why are you weeping? Whom do you seek?" (John 20:15).

Assuming it was the hired man or one of the workmen, Mary of Magdala blubbered, "If you have carried him away, tell me where you have laid him, and I will take him away" (John 20:15). All Mary wanted to do was to give Jesus' corpse a decent burial. She obviously was not hoping for any more than a last look at Jesus' body and the opportunity to set the spices next to it as a gesture of respect and appreciation.

"Mary!" the Stranger said.

Her own name! And spoken by a familiar voice. With the tone she knew so well!

Mary Magdalene turned. Blinking through her tears, looked and saw Jesus!

"Teacher!" she exclaimed, addressing him by the respectful but affectionate term she and Jesus' followers always used.

Mary of Magdala, ecstatically happy, rushed toward the risen, living Jesus Christ. The first to be confronted by the resurrected Lord, this woman forgot all inhibitions about touching a rabbi and joyously reached out her hands to take hold of Jesus. Jesus, she knew, *lives!*

Even today, many church people secretly think that the Resurrection was some sort of body-snatching or disappearing act. Most get only as far as the empty tomb. They can subscribe to Jesus' act of dying on the cross as a noble gesture of self-sacrifice (thereby reducing him to the category of other martyrs like Socrates). These same church people, and hosts of other admirers of Jesus the human Superstar, often speak feelingly of loving others.

Inevitably, however, they all end with a slushy sentimentalism. Patrons of a dead teacher, they romanticize his life and teaching. Expecting the world to turn into an instant Woodstock by burbling about love, they are well-intentioned fans of the world's greatest—and deadest—folk hero.

In a sense, every great religious figure in history is a sort of folk hero. Moses, Buddha, Zoroaster, Confucius, Lao-tzu and Mohammed all fall into this category. So do Gandhi and Martin Luther King, Jr. So also the pseudoreligious folk heroes, including Marx, Lenin and Che Guevara, Lincoln, Malcolm X and the Kennedy brothers. In death, each of these has even become a little larger than life. The point still remains, though, that they are all dead.

Jesus is alive! Give him whatever accolade you wish, but do not venerate him as one on a list of dead folk heroes. Don't even try to label him the greatest hero. Or the greatest this or that or greatest anything, without acknowledging his presence as your living contemporary!

The real meaning of the gospel is Jesus Christ is alive! Mary Magdalene and the other women were the first to learn this gloom-shattering, life-instilling news.

Mary of Magdala rushed to find the others. Excitedly, the first to know personally that Jesus lives announced, "I have seen the Lord!" (John 20:18).

In a sense, the first Christian sermon was preached not by a man but by a woman. "I have seen the Lord!" still stands as the most compelling piece of personal testimony. Whether by prominent pulpiteer or plain maid from Magdala, every effort at preaching must carry the authenticating announcement that the speaker has had firsthand experience with the risen Christ.

If, as many point out, every act, gesture and word is a form of communication, we all are constantly communicating or preaching something. Since we all are in that sense "preachers" are we letting others know that the Lord is alive? "I have seen the Lord!" can be communicated in countless ways.

Jesus Christ continues to surprise us by making himself known to us just when we expect nothing. He startles us, persists in giving evidence of his empowering presence.

Our response?

Communicate that we *have seen the Lord.* We the church have the greatest show-and-tell news of all time!